Presented to:

_____

From:

_____

Date:

_____

365 Devotions for Finding Rest

by Christina M. Vinson

ZONDERVAN®

365 Devotions for Finding Rest
Copyright © 2016 by Zondervan

Requests for information should be addressed to:
Zondervan, 3900 Sparks Dr. SE, Grand Rapids, Michigan 49546

ISBN 9780310083535

Introduction

Rest. What happens when you hear that word? Do you immediately dismiss the idea, thinking it will never happen for you? *After all,* you think, *my life is too busy for me to take a break and rest.* Or does your heart cry out in longing? Does your body crave a reprieve from the hustle and bustle of your days? Does your entire being desperately desire rest?

These days, rest can seem elusive. It appears more like a mirage than something we can fully experience, and when we do experience some sort of rest, it often feels too short. In between deadlines at work, demanding schedules, young children, busy teens, elderly parents, friends, and bills that need to be paid, we've lost our ability to rest well. We are in overdrive. We run to and from meetings and obligations, scarfing down a hurried dinner. We say yes to volunteering in the community and serving at church because it feels wrong to say no. And we collapse on the couch at the end of the day, seeking nothing more than a way to numb our tired, aching brains. Does this sound familiar, friend?

There is good news. There is hope. There is rest—deep, fulfilling, life-giving rest that you truly can have to the fullest. Yes, *you.*

If you're searching for a way to rest—if you're looking to satisfy the deep, God-given yearning in your soul and to quiet the buzzing in your mind that comes from too much activity and not enough downtime—this devotional is for you.

The Lord Jesus spoke candidly about the topic of rest. He knew that we humans would struggle over and over to get the rest we need. That's why, in Matthew 11:28–29, He said, "Come to me, all who labor and are heavy laden, and I will give you rest. Take my yoke upon you, and learn from me, for I am gentle and lowly in heart, and you will find rest for your souls" (ESV). Doesn't that sound wonderful? Jesus speaks truth—and only truth. When He says He will give you rest, He means it. When He says you will find rest for your soul, you will.

So take a deep breath, relax your shoulders, and let your thoughts unwind. Before beginning this journey, ask the Lord to reveal Himself and His truth to you like never before. And ask Him to show you how to live a restful life 365 days of the year.

May you approach each day with renewed hope for rest. May you breathe deeply. May you grasp the life-changing importance of stillness. May you experience the Lord and His deep love for you. May you find rest for your soul.

JANUARY

In peace I will lie down and sleep,
for you alone, Lord,
make me dwell in safety.

—Psalm 4:8

Resolve to Rest

Restore to me the joy of your salvation and grant me a willing spirit, to sustain me.

—Psalm 51:12

Have you thought about any New Year's resolutions? They often include things like losing weight, quitting a bad habit, learning something new, getting out of debt, volunteering, or eating healthier. These are all wonderful goals, but there's one important item that's often overlooked when the clock strikes midnight and the year begins again: rest.

Sometimes we get so busy improving our lives and ourselves that we forget we need rest. Even the Lord rested at the end of His week of creation. As you ponder your resolutions, consider making this year about rest. Commit to spending quiet time with the Lord for fifteen minutes every morning. Try to find two hours of free time every weekend simply to reflect, relax, and rejuvenate. Instead of jetting around the world, why not spend your vacation at home?

Rest is not laziness, nor is it for the fainthearted; it is necessary. Rest is within your reach, and it can be yours this year.

Father God, as I begin another year, will You show me how to rest anew?

Intentional Rest

Jesus often withdrew to lonely places and prayed.

—Luke 5:16

R est doesn't just fall into your lap, and it won't tap you on your shoulder during a busy day. Rest, more often than not, needs to be sought out. It needs to be carved into each day, week, and month, and it needs to be intentional.

Think about your daily schedule. Do you have a slot specifically for rest? You may have a time for picking up the kids, attending book club, making dinner, or working, but is the word *rest* a foreign concept?

Today's culture is busy. Your life is busy. But that doesn't mean you cannot rest; it just needs to be added to your calendar. Just as you make time to see friends or go on a weekend getaway, rest needs to be scheduled. Try getting up fifteen minutes earlier to sit in the quiet. Instead of browsing social media, take a walk outside and breathe deeply. Seek rest, and you will be rewarded—mind, body, and soul.

Lord, help me set aside time each day for rest, even when it seems impossible.

Rest from the List

Whether you turn to the right or to the left, your ears will hear a voice behind you, saying, "This is the way; walk in it."

—Isaiah 30:21

It's always a good feeling to fall into bed at the end of the day with your to-do list neatly checked off, laundry folded and put away, and desk free of clutter. Finishing the list feels good. And it's good to focus and work hard, but not if you're obsessed with "the list."

If you're basing the quality of your day on the number of items checked off your list, that's not truly living. Take an occasional break from the list. Let the grass go unmowed for a week. Skip making the bed. Leave work five minutes early to spend five extra minutes at home. It might feel counterintuitive, but good things are often born from going against the grain.

Remind yourself that life isn't about a list. God won't be shaking His head at you if your day only consists of loving those around you. Let yourself rest. The list will wait.

Lord, help me focus more on loving You and doing my best—and less on the list.

Rest in the Midst of Despair

You gave abundant showers, O God; you refreshed your weary inheritance.

—Psalm 68:9

Is your heart downcast? Why do you feel troubled? This world has so much heartache. Our families carry wounds, friends let us down, loved ones pass away, and it may seem as if life is too hard to handle. We live in a broken world. And we love among broken people.

Perhaps today you are trying your best to fight against despair, but your prayers feel heavy. The weight of this struggle is dragging you down—and you're not sure if you have enough strength to get back up. You feel tired and discouraged.

Take heart, for the Lord *will* rescue you. You can let that burden slide off your back; He promises to carry your heartache, your shame, and your sorrows. In the middle of this storm, remember that God promises to never leave or forsake you—and He means it. Find rest, dear one, in Christ alone.

Lord, I'm no match for this life's trials. Please give me rest and comfort me with Your presence.

Rest from Expectations

Because of the LORD's great love we are not consumed, for his compassions never fail. They are new every morning; great is your faithfulness.

—Lamentations 3:22–23

Now that New Year's celebrations have fizzled out, the ball has dropped, and a new year has begun, life can seem a little less fresh. Perhaps you've already blown your New Year's resolution: that chocolate was a little too tempting, the gym just seems impossible at 5 a.m., or you're simply too busy to take a break from being busy.

Maybe you've spoken harshly to your family too many times. Or perhaps you've already had several disappointments come your way. A brand-new start can feel wonderfully shiny and new until you realize that, in many ways, a new year is less of a beginning and more of a continuation.

Even if you're already disappointed in this year, be encouraged: God's mercies are new every morning, and our slates are wiped clean every day. Release those expectations from your clenched fists and start anew—today, tomorrow, and the next day.

God, help me to be gracious with myself, just as You are gracious with me.

Rest in Winter

I know what it is to be in need, and I know what it is to have plenty. I have learned the secret of being content in any and every situation, whether well fed or hungry, whether living in plenty or in want.

—Philippians 4:12

Each season brings something new. Spring is full of crocus buds and robins, summer slips in with bright sunshine and swimming, fall brings armfuls of colorful leaves, and winter bursts with holidays and snow days.

Whether you love the cooler winter temperatures or can't wait until the thermometer reads ninety, it's important to find rest in each season. Often the busyness of the holidays, the pull of a million different obligations, and the limit of twenty-four hours in a day can get in the way of a restful winter. Allow yourself rest this winter. Take a walk in the brisk air, sit by the fireplace with a cup of coffee, take a hot bath, or read a book underneath a pile of blankets.

Winter is a time to rest and rejuvenate. While it's cold outside, embrace the rest you find in the warmth and comfort of your home.

Lord, may this winter be a season of true rest and refreshment instead of chaos and exhaustion.

Rest from Financial Worries

"Consider the ravens: They do not sow or reap, they have no storeroom or barn; yet God feeds them. And how much more valuable you are than birds!"

—Luke 12:24

Christmas is over and the bills are coming in. Some are perhaps bigger than you were expecting, and as you read them, your spirit begins to deflate. The soaring gas bill reflects your home's warmth during frigid temperatures, the credit card bill reminds you of the winter coats needed to keep your family warm, and the repair bill to fix your car's heating is cringe-worthy.

Are you worrying about finances? Is your neck knotting with stress? Remember, the Lord wants you to give Him every burden and every concern—from the biggest to the smallest. Today, confess your worry to Him. He is the ultimate Provider, and He promises to take care of His children. Take a deep breath and remember that God wants you to be free from worry, even if your bank account looks bleak. Trust in Him.

God, I put my trust in You, the Provider of all good things. You will not desert me.

Begin with Rest

"I will refresh the weary and satisfy the faint."

—Jeremiah 31:25

When your alarm goes off that first day of the week, you may be tempted to hit *snooze*. It can't be the workweek already, can it? Even if you love your job, starting a new week is sometimes difficult, especially if you've had a busy weekend.

While you can't go back and relive your weekend in a more restful manner, you can ensure that your week begins restfully. Today, instead of getting lunch with your colleagues, maybe you need to drive to the park and eat in solitude. If your toddler takes a nap, skip cleaning the kitchen and take one too. Rest can be found in tiny opportunities throughout your day, and those moments can add up. Look for opportunities to rest, soak them up, and use them well. Rest is available in this day; you just need to look for it.

Lord, refresh my spirit and open my eyes to opportunities for rest. May I use them well.

Rest in God's Love

*Be still before the L*ORD *and wait patiently for him.*

—Psalm 37:7

There is nothing you can do to make God love you more—or less. Many people feel they must earn God's love. They think the more involved they are in their church, community, or homeless shelter, the more God will love them. But that isn't true, and if you're not careful, this attitude can let exhaustion creep in and take over.

Church, community, and serving—all those things are good, but they won't make God's love for you grow. Be realistic with yourself and your limits. If you have the time and energy to do more, then, by all means, become more involved. But if the thought of one more thing makes you want to cry, don't feel any guilt or shame. You cannot earn God's love by being busier. The best things you can do for your relationship with Him are to sit in His presence, study His Word, and communicate with Him. Rest in that truth today.

Thank You, Father, for Your unshakable and unchangeable love.

Rest from a Picture-Perfect Life

What do people get for all the toil and anxious striving with which they labor under the sun?

—Ecclesiastes 2:22

Social media can be fun, but it also can be harmful. If you find yourself trying to match your life to what you see online, your efforts will be futile, dear friend. Whether it's on Facebook or Instagram, Snapchat or Twitter, these are only snapshots and sound bites of another's life. They may truly be representative of only one minute out of someone's day.

If you're trying to make your life look picture-perfect, take a rest. Instead of seeing yourself through the lens of someone else's camera, experience your life. It may be messy, broken, tear-stained, and tough. But there are also moments that make you laugh out loud and shout with joy, holy moments that remain engrained in your mind forever. It's your life, your family, and your home—in all its glorious imperfection. Life doesn't need to be photo-worthy to be worth a great deal. Walk away from the pressure of a picture-perfect life, and find rest. You'll be glad you did.

Remind me, Jesus, that this life really is about loving and pleasing You today.

Rest in True Friends

A generous person will prosper; whoever refreshes others will be refreshed.

—Proverbs 11:25

Do you have friends you are constantly trying to impress? Are any friendships in your life based on performance and appearance rather than true acceptance? If so, dear one, listen to these words: these are not true friends. Friendships should feel like a safe place to bare your heart, and not a competition or audition. If yours don't allow you to let your guard down and confess your flaws, and if they don't bring you encouragement, then they may not be the type of friendships you need in your life.

You shouldn't need to strive for acceptance in friendships. They do take work and care, certainly, but you don't need to prove yourself time and time again. True friends love you for who you are; they allow your heart to feel at rest.

Today, think of friends in your life who provide you with true rest, and thank the Lord for bringing them into your life.

Thank You, Lord, for blessing me with true friendships. May I never take them for granted.

Saying No

God is not a God of disorder but of peace.

—1 Corinthians 14:33

No. The word is only two letters long, but it is very difficult to say. Saying no could mean missing out on experiences, serving, fun evenings with friends, or even ministry opportunities. Saying no has a negative connotation—perhaps because it's so hard to hear that word ourselves.

Saying yes is much easier. It makes others happy. It lightens someone else's load, gets you a promotion, and makes you look like a better person. But sometimes the best answer is *not* yes.

In your search for rest, practice saying no. When your plate is too full and your brain is going in a million different directions, it's probably time to say no. You will find space to breathe and time to live your life instead of just getting through, day by day. And it will get easier. Saying no is actually saying yes to the people and things most important to you.

Lord, help me discern when to say yes and when to say no.

Give Yourself Grace

The LORD make his face shine on you and be gracious to you; the
LORD turn his face toward you and give you peace.

—Numbers 6:25–26

We are our own worst critics. When you mess up during a work presentation, or yell at your children, or put your foot in your mouth yet again, you're often the one beating yourself up again and again and again. Dear friend, give yourself a little grace.

You don't need to keep replaying your mistakes or reliving your bad moments. You can find comfort in the Savior who washes you clean, over and over. He does not hold any resentment toward you, and you can breathe deeply knowing you are loved—flaws and all. So revel in the fact that you are covered with grace. And when you begin chastising yourself, when those words of self-condemnation ring in your ears, try to see yourself through the eyes of your loving Father.

Give yourself grace, and rest in the knowledge that He removes *all* your sins from you gladly and willingly.

Lord, Your forgiveness knows no bounds. Teach me to give myself
grace.

Rest for the Sabbath

Yes, my soul, find rest in God; my hope comes from him.

—Psalm 62:5

Sunday is commonly known as a day of rest. It's a day to stop work, be with family, and enjoy time away from the office. But how many of us actually treat this day like a Sabbath? For many families, Sunday mornings are full of rushing: trying to get the kids dressed and out the door, trying to get to church on time, and all the while, feeling a bit frazzled.

What would it take to make your Sundays less stressful and more celebratory? Maybe you need a break from laundry, making meals, or checking off to-do lists. Perhaps you want a leisurely morning with bacon, pancakes, and pajamas before church. Whatever feels the most restful, try to find a way to make it part of your day this Sunday. Let your soul breathe and your shoulders un-tense. This is a day the Lord has made; rejoice, be glad, and celebrate this day in rest.

Quiet my heart and my mind today, Lord. Help me honor You in this day of rest.

When Rest Seems Far Away

"Let anyone who is thirsty come to me and drink."

—John 7:37

If the word *rest* seems like a faraway, outlandish concept, these words are for you. Rest must be sought out and integrated into your life. When you aren't getting enough rest, it affects you mentally, emotionally, spiritually, and physically. *But how can I fit rest into my life?* you wonder.

When something seems far away, you need to begin walking toward it. Today, take one small step toward rest. It may mean saying no to something you'd normally say yes to. It may be putting the kids to bed twenty minutes early so you can have a few minutes alone, or it may be choosing to take a five-minute walk around your office building instead of chatting by the coffeemaker. Rest can come early in the morning or late at night—or even in a mid-afternoon reprieve with a hot cup of tea.

Over time, small steps can take you even faraway places, and rest isn't as far away as you may think.

Father, help me take one or two small steps toward rest today.

A Mind-Set of Rest

He gives strength to the weary and increases the power of the weak.
—Isaiah 40:29

'm so busy! How often have you uttered those words in the past year, month, week, or even day? Some wear busyness as a badge of honor, while others wear it as a burden. Either way, we need rest—whether it's easy to admit or not.

Why not try to have a mind-set of rest instead of busyness? When your calendar is filling up with obligations, it can be easy to try to cram as much as possible into your seven-day week. Instead, ask yourself what would be most life-giving to you and your family. If the thought of serving on one more board, or hosting one more party, or squeezing in one more event leaves you feeling deflated, then say no.

Choose a mind-set of rest. It's okay to be selective about what you add to your calendar. Let rest frame your week instead of busyness. It will do you worlds of good.

Lord, remind me to have a mind-set of rest today and throughout this week.

Rest from Health Worries

The LORD sustains them on their sickbed and restores them from their bed of illness.

—Psalm 41:3

You probably know someone who is struggling with health issues. That person might even be you. Because this world is broken, our bodies simply are not perfect. People suffer with cancer, chronic pain, depression, and more, and it can affect every moment of the day and night.

Whether it's your own battle or that of a loved one, failing health brings fear with it. From fighting with insurance, to wondering if the pain will ever end, to begging God for healing, health troubles can be a constant burden.

Does this sound familiar? Dear one, you have been carrying a heavy load. There are not always answers, but there is truth in this statement: the Lord cares for you. He cares for your family and friends. And He wants you to drop this burden at the foot of the cross and rest awhile. Rest from your deepest fears and troubles by simply coming to Him.

Lord, my burden is heavy. I need Your help and healing and comfort. Come quickly and rescue me.

Take Time for You

A heart at peace gives life to the body.

—Proverbs 14:30

What brings you to life and makes you smile? Is it a weekend spent camping under the stars? Is it kneading dough and watching it rise? Maybe it's writing or playing music. These things that make you smile are important to living a full life. If your days are simply spent working, sleeping, and paying the bills, it's time for a change. It's time to focus on you—not because the world revolves around you, but because we all need some self-care once in a while.

What is that thing that fills you with joy? Resolve to do it—even in a small way—this week. If you don't have time for a camping trip, take a walk in the closest green space. Maybe you can't afford a day at the spa, but why not take a relaxing bath? You need time for yourself. Treat yourself to some rest today.

Remind me to take time for myself, Father. May it be a time of rich communion with You.

Rest from Comparison

When they measure themselves by one another and compare themselves with one another, they are without understanding.
—2 Corinthians 10:12 ESV

We all do it. We compare homes, kids, physical appearances, and our ability to "do it all." We compare personalities, faith, possessions, talents, and money—and the only result is an envious, ungrateful heart.

Comparison may begin innocently enough, but it can easily take over your thoughts—and, consequently, your actions.

Do you want to be freed from the trap of comparison? Instead of focusing on what you do not have, be grateful for all that you do have. Every morning, list a few things you are grateful for, whether it's your light-filled home, your ability to make others laugh, or the freckles that pop out on your face in the summer. The more you open your eyes to all you have, the less likely you'll be to dwell on what you don't have. Freedom from comparison *is* possible, and with it comes the fresh air of rest and contentment.

I struggle with comparison, Lord, and become ungrateful. Give me eyes to see all Your blessings.

When You're Weary

My soul is weary with sorrow; strengthen me according to your word.

—Psalm 119:28

When you're weary, everything is hard. Getting up in the morning is hard; being patient is hard; excelling at work is hard. Bone-deep weariness can leave you feeling wrung out and hopeless. Weary traveler, you *can* find rest.

God knows that your energy is spent and that the thought of living the rest of your life in this kind of exhaustion makes you want to weep. And He also knows exactly how you feel. If you're feeling deeply weary today, ask for help. You don't have to do it all, and the truth is, you *can't* do it all.

Call your closest friend, and ask for help. Ask a church member or family member; tell your spouse (or your boss, or your teammate) you need a break. When you're weary, don't force yourself to keep going in hopes that you'll find rest eventually. Find rest now. Ask for help.

Lord, I am utterly exhausted. Please send people my way to help me find rest.

Invite the Lord In

The LORD will fight for you; you need only to be still.

—Exodus 14:14

The weekend is finally here, but when you look at your list of things to do, your heart sinks. Laundry and carpooling, cleaning and volunteering, budgeting and fixing the toilet—you can practically see the weekend disappear before your eyes. You're already dreading Monday, knowing you'll be just as tired—if not more so—once it arrives.

Are your weekends even fuller than your weekdays? Do you feel exhausted thinking about what's to come? Dear friend, invite the Lord in. He is the breath of life you're longing for. He can give you rest even when it looks as if there's no rest to be found. *Invite the Lord into your weekend.*

Ask Him to show you how to approach your time. Ask Him to give you clear direction on what to keep in your weekend—and what needs to be weeded out. His presence in your few days of rest can and will make a world of difference.

Father, come into my weekend; show me how to use these days to honor You.

Finding Rest in New Beginnings

The boundary lines have fallen for me in pleasant places; surely I have a delightful inheritance.

—Psalm 16:6

If you've ever moved into a new house, gone to a new school, traveled to a new city, or made a new friend, you know *new* can be very exciting. You have a new space to decorate, new people to meet, and new spaces to explore—and of course you want to do it all right now.

Pace yourself, dear friend. New beginnings are fresh and invigorating, but you need to be sure you don't burn out. Your house will eventually feel like home, and if your new friends are real friends, they'll stick around. Don't get so caught up in the newness that you lose sight of what a restful life looks like. Certainly have fun, but also be sure to set aside time to reflect on the good gifts God has given you. He is delighted to bless you, and He deserves your grateful praise.

Lord, You are a God who delights in Your children, and I'm so grateful for Your goodness to me.

Giving Worry to the Lord

"Seek his kingdom, and these things will be given to you as well."
—Luke 12:31

When you're worried, the stress can easily take over your life. Your thoughts drift in conversation, your heart beats faster, and you feel anxious and overwhelmed.

What is it that you're anxious about today? Is it money? Fitting in with others? Finding a spouse? Difficulties with your job? Current events on the news?

Rest assured, the Lord knows your worries and anxieties. He hears you when you're afraid and hurting, and He wants to take this burden you're carrying. Cry out to Him today. Be specific, and ask Him to free you from your anxiety. His response may not be instant—you might not even feel very different at first—but you can be sure that the Lord is moving heaven and earth to rescue you. All you need to do is call out to Him. Give Jesus your worry today. It's never too much for Him to handle, and He will give you rest.

Please help me release my worries to You, Lord. Remind me that You're in control.

Stop and See the Beauty

Will you not revive us again, that your people may rejoice in you?
—Psalm 85:6

Stop and smell the roses is a saying you've probably heard before, but do you ever actually do it? All of creation beckons you to stop hurrying and, instead, to notice the beauty around you—the beauty that's so easy to miss as you scurry on by.

We are all guilty of this. How often do you drive to work not even noticing the sunrise? In the grocery store, do you ever pause to admire the rows of juicy, purple grapes or the cheerful bouquets of flowers? It's easy to say, "Stop and smell the roses," but it's much harder to actually do it.

Today, and throughout your day, challenge yourself to slow down and notice the beauty around you. You may feel as if you don't have the time, but the simple act of slowing down, even for a moment, can bring fresh perspective. Stop and smell the roses today.

Remind me, Lord, even in my busiest moments, to slow down and notice the beauty around me.

Don't Stay Quiet

Wise friends make you wise.

—Proverbs 13:20 CEV

How often does someone confess a struggle, a hardship, or a disappointment in their life, and you respond with, "I had no idea"? If you're like most people, it happens a lot. In our culture, we so often put on a brave face—and we're so good at it—that no one knows the battle within.

Do your friends and family know you are craving more rest in your life? If not, tell them. By keeping quiet, you are only hurting yourself. But by letting friends into your life to help you, you are cultivating rest.

Today, don't be afraid to ask others to help you in your quest to rest more fully, deeply, and intentionally. Rest can be yours—but sometimes you just might need a little help from your friends.

Lord, please fill my life with people who will help me find rest instead of busyness, joy instead of stress.

Rest from Service

As Jesus and his disciples were on their way, he came to a village where a woman named Martha opened her home to him. She had a sister called Mary, who sat at the Lord's feet listening to what he said.

—Luke 10:38–39

God has called us to serve others. Taking meals to the elderly, teaching Sunday school, leading worship, or coordinating a food drive are all good ways to serve. Serving is important, but when your efforts begin to feel more like a chore than a pleasure, it may be time to re-evaluate how you're serving.

If you're so busy serving that you don't have time to spend with the Lord, or if just looking at your calendar makes you feel exhausted, you may want to take a step back. This isn't a call to stop serving altogether; just be wise with how you're spending your time.

The Lord understands that you need rest. Yes, He uses you while you're serving, but He also uses your times of rest to renew you and make you more fit for His service. It is okay to take a break. Ask the Lord to show you how to find true rest—and then listen to His leading.

Lord, teach me to live a life characterized by both service and rest.

Rest from Overscheduling

The LORD replied, "My Presence will go with you, and I will give you rest."

—Exodus 33:14

It's a place we've all been in: you wanted a slow week, but you've overscheduled yourself. Whether you've taken on too much work, scheduled too many social outings, or said yes when you should have said no, we can all relate.

Sometimes you just have to get through an overscheduled week. Even if your commitments are set in stone, be encouraged—you can still find rest.

Whenever you take a quick timeout to eat lunch, take a shower, or drive to your next event, let your mind and body relax. Take long, deep breaths in the car. Let your shower's hot water wash away the tension. Give thanks for your food, and take a few minutes to simply sit at lunch. No, it probably won't feel as good as a two-hour nap or an afternoon at the spa, but these small moments of rest will refresh you. Wherever and whenever you can, find rest today.

I feel overwhelmed today, Lord. Open up moments of refreshment, and help me use them well.

Called to Sabbath-Rest

*"In six days the L*ORD *made the heavens and the earth, and on the seventh day he rested and was refreshed."*

—Exodus 31:17

God separated light from darkness, formed massive mountaintops, and filled lush valleys with wildflowers. He created kangaroos and puppies, sharks and giraffes, and He tossed stars like confetti across the sky. He formed man from dust and breathed life into him. Then He looked around at this great big world, and He called it good. The Lord could have kept on going, but instead, He rested.

On the seventh day, He didn't create or tweak anything or brainstorm new ideas. No, God rested. He took a break—a well-deserved break—and ceased from doing.

Are you planning to take a break today? There is, of course, that never-ending list of what should be done before a new week begins. But today, you are called to rest. You are called to look around and say, "It is good"—even if much is still undone. The Sabbath is for rest. Embrace this gift this week.

Father God, it is so easy for me to just keep going. Please help me slow down and rest.

Unplug to Rest

The LORD gives strength to his people; the LORD blesses his people with peace.

—Psalm 29:11

We like to stay connected. We like to know where our kids are, what our friends are up to, and what the latest news headlines are. And all this information is available with the touch of a screen.

But staying connected can become an obsession. Do you panic if you don't have your phone? Are you constantly scrolling through your social media feeds? Are you reading news headlines more than your Bible? It's easy to get caught up in the trap of being connected.

To find rest—the kind that refreshes mind, body, and spirit—you may need to unplug. Turn off your phone. Set aside your screens and look, instead, into the eyes of your family. Listen to the wind in the trees, and laugh at a silly joke. Unplugging is hard to do, but it is so beneficial. And once you try it, you may not want to plug back in.

Lord, help me seek rest and refreshment in Your presence, not in online noise and busyness.

Resting with Purpose

Consider the blameless, observe the upright; a future awaits those who seek peace.

—Psalm 37:37

Even if you have an entire day to yourself, it's still possible to feel more tired at the end of the day than when it began. Why? You weren't truly resting.

Resting isn't just sprawling on the couch, watching movies, and eating pizza. While that may bring true rest to some, other people's rest looks different. That rest might come in the form of actually doing something. It just depends on one very important person: you!

For some, resting means not setting an alarm and sleeping until 11 a.m., while others find more rest by waking up early and watching the sunrise. Think about what makes you feel the most vibrant—and then do that. Because when you're not resting with purpose, you won't find that deep wellspring of contentment when the day is through. Instead, you'll wish for another day, and another, and another. Hike, fish, sew, bake, nap, or go to the library—whatever it is, do it purposefully.

Lord, I crave rest, but I squander away my opportunities to rest. Teach me to rest intentionally.

Rest from Consumerism

Keep your lives free from the love of money and be content with what you have, because God has said, "Never will I leave you; never will I forsake you."

—Hebrews 13:5

If you battle against wanting to buy, buy, and buy some more, you're not alone. Consumerism is a real struggle for many. Advertisements, social media, and simply the act of living all stir up desires for more.

Now that the holidays are past and the Christmas presents are long since unwrapped, you might feel an urge to shop. When you see an ad for a flash sale or steep discount, you may go running for your credit card. But stop and think first: what would it look like to rest from consumerism?

It looks different for everyone, but here are a few ideas. Buy nothing except necessities for two weeks. Avoid social media and other places where ads are prominent. Ask your friends to hold you accountable. Buying isn't bad, but when wanting more consumes you, it also steals your contentment. Have hope; with Christ, you can overcome all things. And without the idol of consumerism, your life will be more restful.

I am envious of others, Lord, and so I buy more. Please fill me with contentment instead.

FEBRUARY

The LORD replied, "My Presence will go with you, and I will give you rest."

—Exodus 33:14

Rest in Joy

May the God of hope fill you with all joy and peace as you trust in him, so that you may overflow with hope by the power of the Holy Spirit.

—Romans 15:13

Joy is contagious, isn't it? It feels good to be around people who exude a deep-rooted joy. And interestingly, a life full of joy is a life full of rest and trust in God. True joy isn't dependent on circumstances, or personality, or temperament. Joy can be found by anyone.

When you're joyful, you rise above the circumstances around you. You might be in the middle of a difficult relationship, or you may have lost a loved one. Your job may be crummy, or your finances bleak, but joy isn't contingent on any of those things. Joy is found in the Lord.

Joy knows that nothing is too difficult for God. He is near and ready to help in your time of need. He will never leave or forsake you. Joy is more than huge, toothy smiles or constant laughter; joy is believing that the Lord's strength is greater than any trial. Choose joy today, and find rest.

I want that joy, Father—Your joy. Help me rise above my struggles and find true joy.

Rest from Fear About the Future

"Do not worry about tomorrow."

—Matthew 6:34

God knows the future—how long you will live, whom you will love, every triumph, and every failure. He is intricately involved in every single moment of your life, and He is working each of those moments together for His glory. Even so, the future can still be scary.

That's because—for us humans—the future is uncertain. No one knows when this life will end, if that loved one will survive the cancer, or if a child will make good choices. Nobody can predict the job market or stock market or when natural disasters and national tragedies will strike.

No, you can't know the future, but the One who calls you His beloved child does know. The One who calms your fears and wipes away your tears knows what you will need to face that future. Find comfort and rest from fear in knowing that the One who holds the future in His hands also holds you.

Father, I am often afraid of the future. Remind me that You hold the future—and me—in Your hands.

Content at Home

Better the little that the righteous have than the wealth of many wicked.

—Psalm 37:16

Is it hard for you to be content in your home? Whether it's an apartment with roommates, a house with three kids, or a condo by the ocean, home is the place we lay our heads at night. And sometimes it's the place we critique the most.

Your furniture may be fine, but your neighbor's new leather sofa makes yours suddenly look shabby. You don't mind being squeezed into a two-bedroom duplex until your sister buys a six-bedroom home. Your outdated kitchen cooks meals perfectly well, but when you see your colleague's state-of-the-art appliances, it just doesn't seem to do the job.

Contentment is hard. Even at home in the garden of Eden, Adam and Eve wanted more. And since then, the world has been broken. No, your home will never be perfect, and that's okay. Find contentment in your home—flaws and all—and find a better night's rest at the end of the day.

Jesus, instead of seeing my home's flaws, help me see it with a grateful heart.

Letting Yourself Rest

In peace I will lie down and sleep, for you alone, LORD, make me dwell in safety.

—Psalm 4:8

The person getting between you and rest is often someone you know really well: yourself. Does this ring true in your life? Thinking about rest, wanting a break, dreaming of a nap—these can all lead to feelings of guilt or shame. Perhaps you're comparing yourself to those people who just keep going and going and going, never seeming to need rest. Or perhaps you feel guilty about not being able to "do it all."

Want to know something encouraging? When God created the world, He set aside one full day to rest. The God who flung stars into the sky and poured water into the oceans also took time to stop and enjoy what He had made.

Just as the God of all creation rested, you can let yourself rest too. It doesn't mean you're weak. It means you are listening to your body and understanding your limits—and you're doing one of the best things you can do: resting.

Lord, when I feel guilty about needing rest, remind me that You want me to rest.

Rest in Who You Are

Return to your rest, my soul, for the LORD has been good to you.
—Psalm 116:7

There are untold numbers of products, procedures, books, and seminars that promise to make you better—more beautiful, more youthful, more confident, more financially stable. With all of that bombarding us, we can easily become discontented with who we are.

Some days you just need to remember that you're a child of God. He created you with quirks, talents, and a one-of-a-kind personality. You are uniquely you. While it's good to work toward goals and being your best, it's also important to remember that who you are is enough.

When you look in the mirror today, or compare yourself to someone else, or wish you were somehow different, take a moment to tell yourself this: *I am enough.* God loves you simply because you are you. You don't have to become someone else in order for God to love you. Remember that you are enough, and rest in that truth today.

Lord, help me find rest in knowing that You love me simply because I am Your child.

Rest from Fear of Rejection

There is now no condemnation for those who are in Christ Jesus,
because through Christ Jesus the law of the Spirit who gives life has
set you free from the law of sin and death.

—Romans 8:1–2

We all want to be loved, to be admired, and to receive applause for our successes. We want to have friends and relationships and the nod of approval from many. We *don't* want to be rejected.

But because we are broken people, rejection will inevitably rear its head. Your boss might not recommend you for the promotion; a budding friendship could turn ugly; you may find yourself left out and uninvited. Rejection happens, and it hurts. You may wonder if you should even keep trying, or if it might be best to simply sit back and let life happen. Fear of rejection is real.

Are you struggling with that fear today? If so, rest in these words from Jesus: "Whoever believes and has decided to trust in Him [as personal Savior and Lord] is not judged [for this one, there is no judgment, no rejection, no condemnation]" (John 3:18 AMP). The Lord won't reject you; He is a safe place to rest.

Father, rejection makes me want to run and hide. Thank You for
never rejecting me.

A Midweek Rest

This is what the LORD says: "Stand at the crossroads and look; ask for the ancient paths, ask where the good way is, and walk in it, and you will find rest for your souls."

—Jeremiah 6:16

The middle of the week marks the halfway point to the weekend, and it is often the busiest time. Work is demanding, everyone seems to be vying for your attention, and you don't see time for a break anytime soon. Finding rest is hard, but it's not impossible.

Instead of thinking, *It's only Wednesday*, why not congratulate yourself on making it to the middle of the week? Rest doesn't always look like a nap and a lazy day; it might be a spur-of-the-moment celebration. What would celebrating midweek look like? Perhaps a pizza night or your favorite takeout can take the place of making dinner. Wake up a little earlier and drive to the coffee shop for a treat. Take a bath instead of a shower, hit the snooze button one more time, or skip the gym one day in favor of curling up with a book.

Finding rest midweek isn't impossible. Allow yourself to celebrate today.

Lord, I want to celebrate today, even if it's in one small way. Help me find rest today.

Choosing Rest over Busyness

Truly he is my rock and my salvation; he is my fortress, I will never be shaken.

—Psalm 62:2

In our culture, being busy is often seen as a positive thing—even an accomplishment. In fact, if you're not busy, people might find it shocking. How, then, do you choose rest in a world focused on full-speed ahead?

It's simple, really. It's all about choice. You can choose to say yes or to say no. And it's all those yeses and nos that make up your life. The choice is yours, and though that thought seems scary, rest assured, the Lord can help you discern when to add more to your life and when to pull back.

Before you say yes, ask yourself if you have the time and energy to add that thing into your schedule. If you don't, it's okay to say no. *No* doesn't have to mean "never"; it can also mean "not now."

Be brave. Say yes when you can and no when you need to. Then you will find rest in this culture of busyness.

I struggle with saying no, Father. Show me how I can find rest in this time of busyness.

Rest in Your Family

Restore us, O God; make your face shine on us, that we may be saved.

—Psalm 80:3

How often do you make time for your family? Whether you're single, have five kids, or have ten grandchildren, time with family is important. There may be times when it feels like a month has gone by, and you've barely looked at your spouse or called your parents. Or perhaps you rush around all day, shuttling between activities and carpooling, but you still don't really know how your kids are doing.

With jam-packed schedules and so many obligations, making time for family can be tricky. Take a few minutes today to slow down and be intentional with just one family member. Read an extra book to your child, or call your dad. Have a late-night conversation with your spouse, a surprise lunch with your daughter, or a quick cup of tea with your mom.

When you make time for your family—even a few minutes—you'll end the day feeling more satisfied, more connected, and more rested.

I want to connect with my family, Lord. Show me creative ways to make time for them.

Rest and Retreat

Whoever dwells in the shelter of the Most High will rest in the shadow of the Almighty.

—Psalm 91:1

The word *retreat* sounds so nice, doesn't it? It brings to mind visions of open skies, mountains, fresh air, and cozy cabins. Retreating sounds relaxing and enticing—but finding a full week or weekend to get away may seem impossible right now.

Close your eyes for a moment and picture your most relaxing activity. It could be sitting on a white sandy beach, swimming in a crystal-clear lake, walking under gently rustling trees, or sitting on a screened-in porch. How do you feel when you think of those places? Calm and content? Relaxed and peaceful?

Today, just for a few moments, pretend you're there. Breathe slowly and deeply. Let your shoulders relax and your fists unclench. Be grateful for these few moments to sit and clear your mind. You may not be able to go on a weeklong retreat, but the efforts you are putting in to find rest will be rewarded.

Thank You, Lord, for those moments throughout the day when You remind me to sit and rest.

Rest from Burdens

"Take my yoke upon you and learn from me, for I am gentle and humble in heart, and you will find rest for your souls."

—Matthew 11:29

Are you weary, discouraged, stressed, or afraid? Does the busyness of your week ahead make you angry instead of excited? Come to the Lord, dear child. He wants all of your mess—your exhaustion, pain, frustration, and sin. He wants to hear you call His name and ask Him for help—and He will be quick to rescue you.

Don't let one more moment come between you and the One who gave His life for you. Call on His name, and ask Him to relieve you of your burdens. In Scripture, Jesus clearly states He wants to give His people rest—not just for a minute or an hour; He wants to give us complete and unending rest.

Jesus doesn't say, "Come to Me when you have everything figured out." He simply says, "Come to Me." Call out His name, and let Him take your burdens away and replace them with His love, joy, peace, and rest.

I can't do this on my own anymore, Lord, and I'm asking You for help. Rescue me with Your rest.

Do It Now

May the favor of the Lord our God rest on us; establish the work of our hands for us—yes, establish the work of our hands.

—Psalm 90:17

'll do it later. We say those words often. Losing weight, updating a resume, writing a letter, calling Mom—these are things that we want to do, but life's busyness gets in the way. Instead of constantly pushing these things aside, why not just do them now?

The unhappiness you feel when looking in the mirror, the nagging guilt of hearing yet another voicemail from your mom—these could all be in the past if you took care of those things now. In many ways, taking care of business now will actually save time by freeing up space in your mind and in your life. You'll be free from feeling guilty, sad, or overwhelmed. And most of all, you will find respite and rest.

What is something you need to do now? Make a plan, and begin today—and you'll find that both your mind and body will rest a little easier.

God, I so often put off important things. Please give me the discipline needed to get them done.

Seeking Physical Rest

*Even youths grow tired and weary, and young men stumble and
fall; but those who hope in the LORD will renew their strength.*

—Isaiah 40:30–31

How are you feeling physically? Does your body feel worn
out? Is fatigue your constant companion? Do you collapse into bed at the end of the day? You need rest, dear
friend, and you need it now.

Listen to your body. Rest is not a sign of weakness; in
fact, recognizing and acting on the need for physical rest
is one of the best things you can do for your body. If you're
utterly exhausted, it's time to slow down.

Find solitude in a quiet place every day. It might be
on your couch in the early morning hours, or it may come
late at night, after everyone else is in bed. Instead of adding one more event to the calendar, add rest. It may mean
saying no—even to some good things—but you'll be saying
yes to rest. Be still in the quiet, let the day's worries roll
off your shoulders, and allow your body and mind to rest.

*Father, help me remember to take advantage of these quiet times
with You.*

Resting in God's Unfailing Love

Praise the LORD! He is good. God's love never fails.

—Psalm 136:1 CEV

February is known for one very specific holiday: Valentine's Day. There are other notable days (Groundhog Day, President's Day, and of course, the Super Bowl), but if you ask anyone what happens in February, you'll hear about sweet candy hearts, roses, and valentines.

This month, as you think about Valentine's Day, what emotions rise to the surface? Love, joy, and excitement? Or longing, grief, apprehension, and rejection? All these emotions can be associated with this day focused on romantic love. It's a day some celebrate and others despise, and it leaves some feeling special and others feeling unloved.

This year, instead of focusing on the romantic side of Valentine's Day, look to the Lord. He is the only One who can truly satisfy your longing for love. He's the only One who will never fail you, and His love is whole and unconditional. Find rest in the sweet promise of God's love for you. It's better than any box of chocolates.

Lord, please help me never to lose sight of the amazing gift of Your unfailing love.

Rest from Fear of Failure

Restore our fortunes, LORD, like streams in the Negev.

—Psalm 126:4

No one likes to fail. But, at some point in our lives, we all do. Maybe you've already snapped at your children three times today, or you completely forgot about that important meeting and didn't prep for it at all. Perhaps you shared someone's secret, did poorly on a test, or forgot your mom's birthday.

Sometimes we're so afraid of failing that we try to be in control of every last detail. We believe complete control is the key to avoiding failure. But this is an illusion because we can never truly be completely in control.

The fact is, you *will* fail. You will mess up and make mistakes. Apologize, forgive yourself, and move on. Don't battle for control; instead, let the Lord guide your steps. Talk with Him throughout the day. And when you fail, watch His grace step in and wash your mistakes away. Don't let fear of failing reign over your life.

I mess up every day, Father. Cover me with Your grace and remind me that You are in control.

Choose Rest over Stress

"In repentance and rest is your salvation, in quietness and trust is your strength."

—Isaiah 30:15

'm so stressed. How often do we hear—and say—that phrase? But stress isn't good, and it's not something to be proud of. For many of us, though, *stressed* is our default state of being.

How do you choose rest in a stressed-out culture? You fight for it. You choose to spend quiet time with the Lord in the morning, even when every inch of you wants to run around getting ready and checking things off your list. You turn to the Lord when you feel overwhelmed, and you ask a friend for help when you're frazzled.

Simply put, you *choose* rest. Rest won't just happen; it must be intentionally and deliberately sought out. And to find it, you must ask the Lord to guide you to it. Give all your fears and worries over to Him. Choosing rest means choosing to rely on the Lord—and He will lead you to rest.

God, when I feel stressed, remind me that I can fully rely on You.

Rest from Information Overload

Submit to God and be at peace with him.

—Job 22:21

We live in an information-saturated world. All we need to do is type something into an Internet search bar, and a plethora of information appears at our fingertips. If you wonder what koala bears eat, or if you want to know the early signs of Alzheimer's, that information is just a few clicks on the keyboard away. As a culture, we have become addicted to information, and we seek it out daily.

Sometimes, however, we need rest from that information overload. Our brains are bombarded with information all day long, from ads that pop up in our browser to texts about impending bad weather. What would it look like for you to rest from seeking information today?

Ask God to help you be at rest with unanswered questions today. After all, do you really need to know right this second what koala bears eat? Give your mind some rest, and allow yourself the refreshment of just being.

When my mind is overloaded with information, Lord, remind me to seek You and Your kingdom first.

Resting Without Guilt

Very early the next morning, Jesus got up and went to a place where he could be alone and pray.

—Mark 1:35 CEV

If you were to commit a whole day to simply resting, would you feel guilty? Many people would. But resting shouldn't go hand in hand with guilt.

Give yourself permission to rest, and enjoy it without piling on guilt. Resting will make you healthier, happier, and more relaxed. In fact, a well-rested person is more productive and successful than a tired, stressed, and overwhelmed person.

If you feel guilty about resting, remember that Jesus rested. He rested so that He could minister more effectively, and He invited His disciples to rest with Him. Even though there were people who wanted to hear Him speak, He drew away from the crowds and made sure His human body was replenished. Rest is essential for your spiritual, emotional, and physical well-being; it should not cause guilt.

Plan a time of rest this week, and enjoy it. Rest is a gift from God!

Lord, I feel guilty when I try to rest. Help me remember that rest is a gift from You.

Resisting the Urge to Overwork

In vain you rise early and stay up late, toiling for food to eat—for he grants sleep to those he loves.

—Psalm 127:2

A 2014 Gallup report revealed some startling findings: Americans with full-time jobs, on average, work 46.7 hours a week. That's almost an entire extra workday. Plus, 40 percent of those surveyed work up to 50 hours a week. We live in a culture where overworking is the norm.

You may be familiar with this tendency. Whether you're just starting out, are newly promoted, or are in a secure job, you can feel a constant pressure to prove yourself. But the question is, do you want to spend your life overworked and with no time for rest?

Most would answer no. We want to know that, at the end of our lives, we'll have loved deeply and lived fully. Dear friend, as much as you can, resist the urge to overwork. Yes, you may receive some pushback. But stand strong, and you'll walk out of the office every day knowing that you chose a full life—not an overworked life.

Lord, help me resist the urge to overwork. I want to focus on living a full life.

Rest in the Evening

By day the Lord directs his love, at night his song is with me—a prayer to the God of my life.

—Psalm 42:8

When you're a child, evenings usually follow a parent-driven routine of bath, bedtime snack, books, and bed. But when you're an adult, you're on your own. There's no one to tell you to take a bath or go to bed. But what if your bedtime looked more like that of a child?

It's easy to sit on the couch and watch mindless television. Often, that's all your mind wants at the end of a long day. But is collapsing in front of the television every night true rest?

Consider incorporating a more childlike routine into your evenings. Unwind with a bath or hot shower. Drink a calming cup of tea. Read a book, talk to a friend, or cuddle with your spouse. Leave your day's worries with God in prayer, and then *go to bed on time*. If you make your evening routine restful, your body will feel nourished and replenished, and rest will start to be a regular, beautiful part of your life.

Teach me, Lord, how to make my evenings more restful and rejuvenating.

Let It Be

For in six days the LORD made the heavens and the earth, the sea, and all that is in them, but he rested on the seventh day. Therefore the LORD blessed the Sabbath day and made it holy.

—Exodus 20:11

When God included the command to rest in the Ten Commandments, He didn't add a disclaimer of "only if you have time for it." The Lord Himself made time for rest after the creation of the world. And for us, rest simply isn't an option.

The mind-set of being constantly busy is considered normal in today's world, but endless busyness is not what the Lord commanded of us. Yes, He wants you to work hard, but He also wants you to rest. He wants you to take a break from the demands of life and recharge. When was the last time you did that?

This week, be sure to follow the Lord's command. Even if there are things left undone, even when items are still on your to-do list, even if it looks as if rest is the *last* thing you should be doing, let it be *first*. Rest anyway. Other things can wait.

Father God, often I ignore Your command to rest. But here I am, Lord; please help me rest.

Choosing Contentment

"Do not work for food that spoils, but for food that endures to eternal life, which the Son of Man will give you."

—John 6:27

Socrates once said, "He who is not contented with what he has, would not be contented with what he would like to have." So often we think that if we just had a new house, different job, new wardrobe, better-behaving kids, more money, or even a different spouse, we would be happier—we would be content. But would we?

Contentment is a choice; it doesn't magically appear. It doesn't automatically come with a new job or a new pair of jeans. If you want contentment—and a rest from feelings of discontent—you must choose it.

Choosing to be content begins with gratitude. If you focus on what you don't have, you immediately become less grateful for all you do have. The Lord knows it's a struggle, and He also wants to untangle you from the trap of discontentment. Call on Him today. Ask Him to give you freedom, contentment, and rest.

Oh, Father, I struggle with being content. Please free me from the trap of discontentment.

Rest in Nature

Let the heavens rejoice, let the earth be glad; let the sea resound,
and all that is in it. Let the fields be jubilant, and everything in
them; let all the trees of the forest sing for joy.

—Psalm 96:11–12

When was the last time you enjoyed the outdoors? And no, walking to your mailbox, your neighbor's house, or your car doesn't count. When the weather is cold, it's difficult to get outside. A warm house is much more enticing than frigid wind, rain, and snow. But being outside in God's creation is important.

Average Americans spend 87 percent of their time indoors and 6 percent of their time in an enclosed vehicle. That's a lot of time inside!

God didn't create nature simply to be seen; He created it to be enjoyed. Challenge yourself to get outside today. If it's chilly, bundle up. Breathe in the fresh air; find a park to explore; admire the birds hopping from branch to branch. Being outside brings with it a special kind of rest that is refreshing to your soul. Rest in the beauty of God's creation today, and praise Him for this beautiful world.

Lord, it's hard to go outside during colder months. Remind me to
rest in Your beautiful creation.

Rest from Perfectionism

I will boast all the more gladly about my weaknesses, so that Christ's power may rest on me.

—2 Corinthians 12:9

Perfection is unattainable. Ever since Adam and Eve sinned in the garden of Eden, life simply has not been perfect. Yet a lot of us seek perfection in our lives. We want a perfect life, perfect marriage, and perfect house. We want to look perfectly put together, and we want to do a perfect job in our workplace. We strive for perfection as though it were attainable, and we end up exhausted.

The good news is that God doesn't demand perfection from you. He knows you can't be perfect, and that's why He sent Jesus to die for you. Jesus was perfect *for* you—in your place. And the best thing you can do is to fall before Him every day, ask Him to lead you, and then follow His leading. You can do everything to the best of your ability, but you'll never be perfect. And that's okay. Rest from perfectionism today.

Father, please remind me that I can rest from perfectionism because Jesus lived a perfect life for me.

Know Yourself

You have looked deep into my heart, LORD, and you know all about me. You know when I am resting or when I am working, and from heaven you discover my thoughts.

—Psalm 139:1–2 CEV

God made each of us unique. You probably know people who are brilliant, funny, outgoing, and reserved. You may be peppy first thing in the morning, or you might be more of a night owl. You might love being the center of attention, or you may prefer watching rather than participating. We are all different people, and our need for rest also differs.

Some may need only five hours of sleep a night, while you need nine or ten to function. Your best friend may need to spend Saturdays in isolation, while you love to go out for breakfast, lunch, and dinner with your friends. If you need more rest than others, it's not a flaw. And if you need less rest than others, don't look down on those who need more.

Know yourself and your capacity for work and rest—and then honor your need for rest.

Show me how much rest I need, Lord, and help me rest accordingly.

The Fear of Falling Behind

"Who of you by worrying can add a single hour to your life? Since you cannot do this very little thing, why do you worry about the rest?"
—Luke 12:25–26

What would happen if you took a day off work? Would your family still function if you went away for one day? Would your ministry fail if you retreated to a quiet place for the weekend? One of our biggest fears about rest is this: if we rest, we'll fall behind. Our competitors will get ahead; our family will fall to pieces; our ministry will be neglected.

Take this to heart, dear friend. When you rest, you are strengthened. Rest energizes you and restores your soul. Rest can only do you good—and you'll return with a new zest for life.

Your world will not end if you take a day off to rest. You may have to work hard before or after, and time off might feel strange, but in the end, you'll be a better worker, parent, and pastor because you took time to recharge. And the Lord *will* bless your efforts to rest.

God, I confess that I'm afraid of falling behind if I take time off. Give me courage to rest.

When Life Is Painful

How long, O LORD? Will you forget me forever? How long will you hide your face from me? . . . But I have trusted in your steadfast love; my heart shall rejoice in your salvation. I will sing to the LORD, because he has dealt bountifully with me.

—Psalm 13:1, 5–6 ESV

The psalmist David made lots of mistakes and suffered the consequences. He often felt far from God, and at times, he even despaired.

Are you going through a painful time in your life? Is your heart broken into a million pieces, and do you wonder if it will ever be whole again? You may be suffering physical pain, or perhaps you've lost a loved one. Maybe you are experiencing depression, or you feel a deep loneliness. There are many ways pain can appear in our lives, and it can feel like an impossible burden. Take heart, dear one, for when life is painful, the Lord is right beside you.

God isn't far away, up in the sky, ignoring you. Rather, He is bearing the pain right along with you. He is wrapping His arms around you and shedding tears with you. Cry out to Him and find rest in His comfort and strength.

How long, O Lord, will I feel this pain? Lift it away and dry my tears.

Rest from Productivity

Unless the LORD builds the house, the builders labor in vain.

—Psalm 127:1

Productivity is a word used proudly. The more we get done in the day or week, the more accomplished we feel. Long workdays are often expected, and working on the weekends is the norm. In a society where productivity is king and rest is dismissed as unnecessary, how do we find respite from the constant going, going, going?

We simply have to do it. *We rest.* We rest without hesitation and without guilt. We take time off from work and obligations to enjoy our families, our God, and His creation. Rest is essential; our culture just doesn't want to admit it.

You may feel as if your world will come crashing down if you're not productive. You might feel as if it's impossible to rest if your to-do list isn't finished. You might even feel lazy or worthless if you take time to rest. Push those thoughts out of your head because rest is essential—God can handle everything else.

God, I am afraid to rest and feel unproductive. Show me that when I rest, the world benefits.

MARCH

Return to your rest, my soul,
for the Lord has been good to you.

—Psalm 116:7

Enjoying God

"You will seek Me and find Me, when you search for Me with all your heart."

—Jeremiah 29:13 NKJV

Imagine your favorite dessert. Is it a warm, gooey brownie straight from the oven or a tangy lemon bar topped with powdered sugar? Maybe it's a slew of Oreos with milk or a cupcake topped with decadent frosting. Now imagine eating your dessert during rush-hour traffic. Your shirt is covered with crumbs; half the Oreos fall under the seat; you choke on the cupcake as traffic slams to a stop. Doesn't sound very enjoyable, does it?

Now picture yourself sitting in your comfiest chair, slowly savoring each bite. That's a completely different experience, isn't it?

Your experience with God is similar. If you hurry through your time with Him, let distraction take over, or try to multitask in your prayer life, you won't enjoy the experience nearly as much. But if you take meaningful, intentional time to enjoy the Lord and His Word, you'll find relief from stress and worries—and you'll find rest.

Help me not to rush my time with You, Lord, but to be more intentional about our time together.

Turn Off Technology, Tune Into Dinnertime

"Be still, and know that I am God."

—Psalm 46:10

Twenty years ago, if you looked around a restaurant, you would see couples, families, and friends talking, laughing, and enjoying being together. Today, however, you'll see many diners on their phones—texting, browsing the Web, and checking their e-mail.

Technology has helped us in many, many ways, and we should be grateful for its role in our lives. But technology shouldn't *be* our life.

Think about your time at the dinner table. Are you engaging with your family or friends? When you're eating solo, are you intentionally enjoying the moment? Or does your dinnertime involve your phone or other device? Are you looking at your screen more than the faces of your family? Instead of enjoying your meal and reveling in the flavors, are you mindlessly scrolling through your social media feeds?

Limiting your interaction with technology at dinnertime will help you connect more with God, yourself, and others—and your eyes and brain will be grateful for the rest.

Help me use dinnertime to be more focused on You and on those around me.

Teaching the Habit of Rest

Start children off on the way they should go, and even when they are old they will not turn from it.

—Proverbs 22:6

Children learn through seeing. They are watching those closest to them: their parents, siblings, friends, and teachers. And like little sponges, they soak up everything you say and do—whether it's beneficial or not.

If you want your children to grow up less stressed, less harried, and not burned out, it's important for you to model a habit of rest. Even if you don't have children, you can be an excellent example to nieces or nephews, students, neighbors, and friends.

A habit of rest needs to be *purposeful*. That means you are diligent in your efforts to find rest. It's not something you can keep putting off; otherwise, neglecting rest will become your habit. Set a goal of resting daily or weekly, and begin this life-giving habit. Model a restful life to those around you, and they will in turn be drawn to a life lived with purposeful rest.

Lord, help me adopt a habit of rest and inspire others to live a more restful life.

Is This Fruitful?

*Walk in a manner worthy of the Lord, fully pleasing to him,
bearing fruit in every good work and increasing in the knowledge
of God.*

—Colossians 1:10 ESV

As Christians, we feel the call to serve. We serve on committees, as elders and deacons, and as teachers. We visit the elderly, bring meals to needy families, and participate in a plethora of other service-related activities. Those are all good things, but just because an opportunity arises doesn't mean you're the one called to do it.

If you need to cut back, ask yourself, *Is this service fruitful? Are we seeing results? Is this a good fit for my season of life? Am I serving out of love or obligation?* Those are tough questions, but when life is speeding by at a record pace, you need to ask them.

Asking these questions may bring relief or nervousness. You might even feel guilt or anxiety about taking something off your plate. But remember: your heavenly Father has the perfect answers. Ask Him to show you where you are needed and where you can step down—and find rest in His answers.

*Father, guide my decisions and show me when I should serve and
when I should rest.*

Guarding Your Time

He leads me beside quiet waters, he refreshes my soul.

—Psalm 23:2–3

If you lead a busy life, you may be craving time to yourself, but you never seem to have any. Your schedule fills up with work, social outings, family, bills, and more. Then, before you know it, you're falling into bed an hour later than you were hoping.

Often, the only way to find time to yourself is to guard it. It needs to be a nonnegotiable, mandatory, rigid part of your day or week. Nothing except an emergency should take its place—even if your friends are having a last-minute movie night, or your child wants to go sledding, or you've just realized you're out of milk. Jealously guard that hour or two just for yourself—those other things can wait—and you'll feel more rested, energized, and calm as a result.

Remember: your time is valuable, so guard it well. You won't regret it.

Remind me to guard my time, Lord, especially in moments of busyness.

Rest Doesn't Let Others Down

*Consider him who endured such opposition from sinners, so that
you will not grow weary and lose heart.*

—Hebrews 12:3

When you rest, you aren't letting other people down.
You may have said no to the extra work project, birthday party invitation, church service opportunity, or other
event. But you said yes to something very important: your
need for rest.

Are you afraid that if you take time out to rest and
rejuvenate yourself, you're going to be viewed as lazy? Do
you feel that everything will fall apart if you aren't there
to control it? Be assured, dear friend, resting will only do
you good. Caring for yourself is just as important as fulfilling others' needs—and you can't be effective at helping
others if your body and mind are utterly exhausted.

Today, remind yourself that if you choose to rest, you're
still choosing well. You are not letting anyone down, and
you are certainly not letting God down. Ask God to help
you see this truth and to rest in it.

*Father, I am afraid to rest because I fear others' disapproval. Please
show me how to rest without fear.*

A Day of Rest

"Tomorrow is to be a day of sabbath rest, a holy sabbath to the LORD."

—Exodus 16:23

Sometimes the most spiritual thing you can do is take a nap. Pastors and speakers have echoed this sentiment through the years, but how often do we follow their advice?

Our body needs physical rest. If we keep pushing and pushing and pushing, we'll burn out at work, we'll burn out at home, and we'll burn out our bodies. Physical rest is necessary for us to function fully and wholly.

Consider taking a nap today. Listening to sermons, teaching Sunday school, or having a family outing are all wonderful and even necessary parts of our Sabbath days, but don't discount the spiritual value of an afternoon nap. Challenge yourself to carve out a naptime today. It may seem self-indulgent, but it can actually be the best thing for your spiritual, physical, and emotional health. When you're napping, you're following the Sabbath command: to rest.

Lord, remind me today that a nap can be a wonderfully spiritual thing to do for my tired body!

Rest in God's Provision

"Do not worry about your life, what you will eat; or about your body, what you will wear. For life is more than food, and the body more than clothes."

—Luke 12:22–23

Even the rich worry about money. Businesses rise and fall every day; there could be a stock market crash or a sudden shift in consumer interest. Even if you have millions in the bank, money can still be a constant source of stress. And those who struggle to make ends meet have even more serious concerns about the money that buys their clothes and the food on their table. Without their income, they could end up homeless.

Money can be worrisome for the rich, the poor, and everyone in between. Would you like a rest from worrying about money? The Lord is willing and able to take away your burden. Whether you are worried about losing money, wondering how in the world to make money, or anxious about your next meal, the Lord understands. And He says, "Do not worry." He knows what you need, and He promises to provide for you. Rest in that promise today.

Father, please take away my worry about money, and replace it with trust in You.

"Come to Me" for Rest

"Come to me, all you who are weary and burdened, and I will give you rest."

—Matthew 11:28

Jesus speaks three words in Matthew 11 that can revolutionize your life: "Come to me."

He specifically calls the weary and burdened—those who are overwhelmed with life, those who are so busy they can't see straight, and those who are simply tired. What does He call them to? *Rest*. Jesus clearly says, "I will give you rest." Notice the Lord doesn't say, "Come to Me when you have a plan for how to rest" or "Come to Me, and I might help you." He says, "Come to me, all you who are weary and burdened, and I will give you rest."

The Lord doesn't want to see you barely holding on. He doesn't care who you are, or what kind of job you have, or what kind of car you drive. He simply wants to make sure you experience soul-renewing rest. Will you come to Him and accept that rest today?

Lord, I come to You now, mess and all, and I ask for the rest that You promise.

Exercise to Rest

I urge you, brothers and sisters, in view of God's mercy, to offer your bodies as a living sacrifice, holy and pleasing to God—this is your true and proper worship.

—Romans 12:1

How can jogging three miles or biking for an hour be restful? Physical exercise may tire out your body, but it does wonderful things—restful things—for your mind. If you are overwhelmed with the demands of today, you may want to consider pulling on your tennis shoes.

Getting your heart rate up, working up a sweat, and pushing yourself physically will actually help you unwind. If you're stressed and try to combat it by moping around the house and eating potato chips, you may actually become even more anxious because your mind is focusing on one thing: stress. When you exercise, however, you're producing more endorphins, getting better sleep, and essentially boosting your energy.

If you feel worn down and discouraged, you may just need to work up a sweat—and through it, you'll find rest.

Creator God, inspire me to take care of my body and find rest for my overwhelmed mind.

Inhale, Exhale, and Release

My heart is not proud, LORD, my eyes are not haughty; I do not concern myself with great matters or things too wonderful for me. But I have calmed and quieted myself.

—Psalm 131:1–2

When you're worried or stressed, your breathing becomes different. Your breaths are small and shallow instead of deep and even, and you engage your shoulders instead of your diaphragm. Your jaw clenches and tightens.

You probably don't have time for a massage or the spa, but you want to feel better. You want your body and mind to feel at rest. That's where inhaling, exhaling, and releasing come in.

If your breathing is shallow, take several deep breaths in a row. Let your breath expand your lungs and move your diaphragm. As you exhale, do so slowly and in a controlled manner. If your jaw is tense, move it back and forth and do some stretches with it; you may feel a little silly, but you will also feel better. Throughout the day, do this breathing and jaw check. If you feel tension, then inhale, exhale, release . . . and rest in your breathing.

Father, remind me to inhale, exhale, and release whenever I feel anxious.

Rest in Today's Triumphs

This is the day which the LORD hath made; we will rejoice and be glad in it.

—Psalm 118:24 KJV

So often, at the end of a day, we feel defeated by everything that we didn't do. We forgot to pick up the dry cleaning, we didn't finish those meeting notes, and we got takeout for dinner again. And our to-do list? It grew.

Instead of focusing on the day's defeats, why not rest in today's triumphs? Grab a pad of paper and write down everything you *did* do—from the smallest to the largest. Maybe you fed all three kids and got them to the bus stop on time. Perhaps you nailed the big presentation at work. Did you encourage a friend, laugh until you cried, or point someone toward Christ today? Write it all down.

Today's defeats can be frustrating, but don't let them dominate your feelings about the day. Rest in today's triumphs. Tomorrow is a new day, but today wasn't a complete waste. Celebrate your triumphs, and rest in knowing that God is glorified by your efforts.

Help me celebrate today's triumphs, God, and rest in the glory they bring Your name.

Rest for a Busy Week

Make your face shine upon your servant, and teach me your statutes.

—Psalm 119:135 ESV

When you look at your calendar, do you ever get a sinking feeling in your stomach? Each morning is filled with work, and every evening has some type of commitment. Sometimes there's not much you can do about having a busy, filled-to-the-brim week. But you can control your response to it. And you can still find rest; it just may look a little different.

Look for pockets of rest. Stuck in the car? Turn on some worship music or simply sit in silence, soaking in the Lord's presence. Do you have back-to-back meetings all day? Take just a few moments in between to practice deep breathing; you'll enter your meetings calmer and more refreshed. If you're serving in your church's Easter production, take a minute beforehand to praise God for His sacrifice.

You may feel weary when you look at the week ahead, but know there is rest waiting for you—even when your calendar is full.

When I am overwhelmed, Father, help me find moments of rest in Your presence.

A Centering Sabbath

*There remains, then, a Sabbath-rest for the people of God; for
anyone who enters God's rest also rests from their works, just as
God did from his.*

—Hebrews 4:9–10

In many ways, Sabbath is a state of being. And in order for
a Sabbath to be a true Sabbath, it needs to be restful—for
the Sabbath was founded on rest.

Not only does the Sabbath help rejuvenate us for the
week ahead, but it also reminds us that the world can go on
without us for a day. It re-centers our hearts on the Lord.
It's a celebration of Him and His care for His people. After
all, God could have told us to work seven days a week, but
out of His kindness, He told us to rest.

If your Sabbath is filled with more doing than resting, it's time to reimagine what it can look like. After all,
a Sabbath should be like a balm for a weary soul. Seek rest
through the Sabbath; it will transform your week in a new,
refreshing, joyful way.

*Lord, I want a Sabbath that refreshes my soul. Show me how to
rest—truly rest—on the Sabbath.*

Start with Grace

It is by grace you have been saved, through faith—and this is not from yourselves, it is the gift of God.

—Ephesians 2:8

Monday can be a dreaded day. It's at the very beginning of the week, and it's the furthest day from the weekend. Often, your Monday sets the tone for the rest of the week. This week, start with a little bit of grace.

As you sit with the Lord, acknowledge that you will make mistakes. Tell Him your worries and fears for the week. Bring every request, big and small, to His throne. Then resolve to give yourself grace.

This will not be a perfect week. You will not be a perfect parent, friend, child, or grandparent. You will mess up in tiny ways and in significant ways. You will have triumphs and failures throughout the week. But there is grace for it all. You have a Father who loves you infinitely, and His mercies are new every single morning. Start your Monday by holding tightly to His hand and resting in His grace.

Jesus, this week, I will make mistakes. But I praise You in advance for Your grace toward me.

Finding Rest in God Alone

Truly my soul finds rest in God; my salvation comes from him.

—Psalm 62:1

When you find yourself exhausted, weary, and yearning for rest, the ultimate question to ask yourself is, *Am I seeking the Lord?* True rest can only come from God. Stretching, retreats, hot baths, and saying no are all great ways to usher rest into our lives, but the Lord is at the core of rest.

As David says in Psalm 62, salvation and rest come from God. You simply need to call His name and ask for help, and then He will guide you toward rest. Be warned: it might be uncomfortable or challenging. God may ask you to give something up, or He may bring sin into light. But in the end, you will find the greatest rest on earth—rest given by God.

Today, ask yourself if you're nurturing your relationship with the Lord. Is He the highest priority in your life? Because true rest is found in Him. Let that be both a comfort and a challenge to you.

Lord, ultimately, You are the One who gives true rest. Lead me closer to You.

Rest in the Unfinished

You will keep in perfect peace those whose minds are steadfast,
because they trust in you.

—Isaiah 26:3

Your body and mind cry, *Go to bed*, but you refuse because there are still half a dozen things to finish up for the day. Sound familiar?

While some tasks must be finished (a work project, feeding the baby, paying a bill), there are many other responsibilities that can be put off for another time.

If you feel exhausted, ask yourself, *Are there negative consequences for not finishing this today?* Then weigh the pros and cons. Sometimes you may just have to push through and finish up. But often, it's simply our pride or stubbornness that stands between us and rest.

Even if things aren't finished, if the house is a mess and the dishes are piled in the sink, even if you aren't finished packing or the room is half-painted, rest is more important. Let yourself off the hook, and allow yourself to rest even if a few things must remain undone.

I want to make rest my priority, Lord. Help me trust that everything
else will fall into place.

Rest in the Risen Christ

"I have come that they may have life, and have it to the full."
—John 10:10

In springtime, Christians remember the life, death, and resurrection of Jesus Christ. The Crucifixion is mourned and celebrated, cherished and illuminated. Yet how often do you live as though you have rest in His finished work? From the cross, Jesus said, "It is finished." He died so that you may have life to the fullest. Now ask yourself: are you living life to the fullest?

Too many of us would answer with a resounding *no*. Life doesn't feel full and joyful; it feels overwhelming. We try to prove ourselves to friends, family, and even God. We find purpose in working for our church, but are we truly living a God-focused life?

Christ died to give you rest and healing so that you wouldn't need to strive for God's approval. His desire isn't for your life to be frantic and hectic; His desire is for you to live a life of joy because of His great gift. Rest in His sacrifice today.

Father, help me seek out a time of rest to remember the sacrifice You made for me.

Cultivating a Restful Home

My people will live in peaceful dwelling places, in secure homes, in undisturbed places of rest.

—Isaiah 32:18

Our homes reflect who we are. Some are perfectly tidy with no clutter in sight. Others have a pot of chili bubbling on the stove, baseball gloves on the tables, and toy cars littering the carpet. Some homes are sleek and fashionable; others are simple and practical. Homes come in all shapes and sizes, but one important aspect to keep in mind is this: is it a home of rest?

Having a home of rest doesn't mean it has to have the comfiest beds or be completely quiet in the evening. A home of rest means you are demonstrating to others that rest is a priority for you. Perhaps you have rules about screen time and phones and bedtimes. Those are good, but a home of rest is, above all, a place of grace, and love, and practiced peace—a place that provides a respite for those weary from the world. Are you cultivating a home of rest?

Dear God, show me how I can bring a sense of peace and rest to my home.

The Promise of Spring

Faithfulness springs forth from the earth, and righteousness looks down from heaven.

—Psalm 85:11

Depending on where you live, March may be a month filled with crocus buds, delicate tree blossoms, and gentle rain showers. Or the ground could still be frozen and covered by a blanket of snow. Or maybe your March looks a lot like the eleven other months of the year: sunny and seventy-five degrees. Whatever spring looks like for you, the concept of the season is the same: life after death.

Be encouraged. Though you may feel exhausted right now, and you may not see any signs of spring, it is coming. It always does. Bare branches will fill with leaves, soil will soften, fruit trees will bloom, and new life will spring out of dry ground.

Rest in the promise of spring. It is on the horizon. Maybe it's not here yet, but it will be soon. Spring is coming—look for it, for the Lord is on the move.

Even in the winter of my soul, I know You are with me, Father. I rest in Your promise of spring.

No Need to Apologize

Then, because so many people were coming and going that they did not even have a chance to eat, he said to them, "Come with me by yourselves to a quiet place and get some rest."

—Mark 6:31

If you told a friend or colleague about a relaxing, restful, absolutely renewing weekend, would you feel the need to apologize? We're often quick to boast about our busyness, but we're hesitant to talk about our need for rest. And then, when we do rest, we often feel as if we've stolen the time.

Dear friend, be relieved of the need to apologize for taking time to rest. You don't need to harbor regrets for tending to your mind, body, and soul. Remember: the Lord didn't apologize for resting after creation, and He commands you to rest—in fact, He *wants* you to rest.

If you're ashamed of resting, be freed from that feeling. Instead, bask in the energy, joy, and freedom from stress that you receive from resting intentionally and well.

Lord, turn my heart toward seeking Your approval instead of worrying what others may think.

Restful Friendships

Two are better than one, because they have a good return for their labor: If either of them falls down, one can help the other up. But pity anyone who falls and has no one to help them up.

—Ecclesiastes 4:9–10

The best of friends make you feel at home. You feel safe seeing them while in your sloppiest clothes and on your messiest days. All pretenses dissolve, and you can tell them anything.

Other friendships might be more difficult. You may feel that you constantly need to prove yourself, that you always need to put your best foot forward, and that you need to cover up any insecurity. Does this describe any of your friendships? Do you feel as if they require constant work to maintain? If so, ask the Lord to bring restful friendships into your life.

As Proverbs 17:17 says, "A friend loves at all times." A friend loves you when you're a blubbering mess and when you confess your mistakes. A friend loves through good times and hard; a true friend doesn't disappear. A friend should bring rest, not stress, to your life. Thank God for your restful friendships today.

Lord, will You bring to my life specific people who are willing to live a life of rest with me?

Rest While Waiting

The peace of God, which transcends all understanding, will guard your hearts and your minds in Christ Jesus.

—Philippians 4:7

Waiting is hard. It requires patience, total trust in the Lord, and more patience. Whether you're waiting for a spouse, a child, an answer from God, or a job, the slow passing of time can feel excruciating. You long to do something. After all, doing something will move things along, right?

Remember that God's plans are perfect. He knows your next step in the most vivid detail. God wants to show you what a beautiful and extravagant story He's weaving together for you, but He also wants you to wait on Him. Waiting sharpens character and strengthens perseverance. It takes away any sense of entitlement and teaches humility.

If you're in a time of waiting, seek the Lord's face. Call to Him when you're discouraged, rest in His promises, and revel in the comfort of His goodness. Find rest in the waiting—the Lord is working in your life. Wait for Him.

This waiting feels so long, Jesus, but I am excited to see the story You're writing for me.

The Idol of More

Godliness with contentment is great gain.

—1 Timothy 6:6

The idol of "more" has been with us since childhood—more Christmas presents, more ice cream, more attention. And "more" remains a huge struggle for many adults in today's world.

Companies spend millions upon millions of dollars to convince you that you need more clothes, more gadgets, more stuff. The more you volunteer at your child's school, the more respect you expect to receive. The more hours you work, the higher your pay. The list of "more" goes on and on.

But here's the truth: we need less—less of "us" and our own needs and wants—and we need more of Him. When we spend more time with Jesus, we are filled and rewarded by becoming more like Him. We become smaller, and He becomes greater. Take time for Jesus today, and find rest from the idol of "more."

Father, I want to become more like Jesus. Give me an unquenchable thirst for more of You.

Finding Rest in Unavailability

The LORD longs to be gracious to you; therefore he will rise up to show you compassion.

—Isaiah 30:18

Tired. Exhausted. Worn out. Overworked. Stressed. Too busy. If those words describe you, it may be time to be unavailable for a bit. You need to create margin and space in your life, and sometimes the only way to do that is by saying no.

You want to help others and be involved. You love feeling needed and productive. But there comes a time when you need to say, "No more."

Consider being "unavailable" for a season. Do your work, and do it well. Love your family and God, and love them well. But everything else may need to go by the wayside for a time. Being unavailable isn't a lifelong status, and it won't cause the world to spin off its axis. Instead, it will create space in your life for you to be refreshed, to pray more, and to love more deeply. Most importantly, you will be able to seek the Lord and find rest by keeping Him first.

Lord, teach me when I should be available and when I should be unavailable.

Your Nightly Rest

On my bed I remember you; I think of you through the watches of the night. Because you are my help, I sing in the shadow of your wings.

—Psalm 63:6–7

Going to bed might seem like an obvious way to rest, but it's easier said than done. If you lead a busy life, evenings may be the only time to connect with your spouse or kids. Evenings might be your only alone-time throughout the day, and if you're an introvert, that's crucial. You might only have time to see friends after work, and if you're an extrovert, you need that social stimulation. And sometimes, the movie or television show you're watching is just too good to turn off.

Those are all valid reasons *not* to go to bed—and they are also why going to bed requires discipline. Observing a set bedtime requires a firm commitment to getting an adequate amount of sleep so that your body isn't physically tired.

Sometimes rest involves sacrifice. Decide on a reasonable hour for bedtime and stick to it. You'll be amazed by how rested you'll feel in the morning.

Lord God, I know I need more sleep. Please give me the discipline to go to bed.

Rest at Mealtime

Every good and perfect gift is from above, coming down from the Father of the heavenly lights, who does not change like shifting shadows.

—James 1:17

Mealtimes are often hectic—whether you're a family juggling the needs of small children, a single parent chasing after teenagers, or just a busy person snatching yet another meal on the run. But finding rest at mealtime is still possible.

Most people eat three meals a day: breakfast, lunch, and dinner. Choose one meal to be your mealtime of rest. That can mean many things: no technology allowed at the table, eating lunch in quiet solitude, taking time to pray as a family before the meal, or even intentionally savoring your food rather than scarfing it down. Above all, make sure you relish mealtime as a chance to sit and enjoy God's provision in a tangible way.

Whether you're eating waffles hot off the griddle, a juicy steak, or a bowl of cold cereal, God has provided for you. Take time during your meal to rest in the knowledge of His goodness toward you.

You are my ultimate Provider, Lord Jesus. You are so good to nourish both my body and soul.

Listening to Find Rest

The LORD came and stood there, calling as at the other times, "Samuel! Samuel!" Then Samuel said, "Speak, for your servant is listening."

—1 Samuel 3:10

Have you ever simply sat quietly with the Lord? Do you ever pause between the requests and complaints in your prayers to hear what He has to say? Listening to the Lord is an important part of a Christian's life. But in our mission to get things done, it's often hard to sit still and listen.

Practice listening to the Lord. After reading this devotion and studying the scripture, sit before the Lord in quiet expectation. Resist the urge to talk, and instead, invite Him to speak to you. You probably won't hear an audible voice, and you may not even be completely sure of what He's saying, but as you practice listening to Him, you'll learn to recognize His still, small voice.

Listening to the Lord is a form of rest. It involves sitting back and waiting for Him to speak. It entails quieting your heart, mind, and spirit, for when you are still, He will answer—and you will find rest.

I want to listen to You, Lord, and not just list all my requests. Speak, Lord; I am listening.

Rest from Seeking Approval

Am I now trying to win the approval of human beings, or of God? Or am I trying to please people? If I were still trying to please people, I would not be a servant of Christ.

—Galatians 1:10

We all love approval. We all love to be loved. It's intoxicating and addictive, and it boosts our self-esteem by leaps and bounds. But too many of us seek others' approval more than we seek God's approval.

When we set out to gain the approval of others, it can turn into a never-ending quest. That's because the minute we earn someone's approval—whether that person is our boss, new friend, spouse, parent, significant other, or teacher—we're off and searching for someone else's too. We want that stamp of approval from everyone, and that can be exhausting.

It's natural to want to be well liked. We want others to think highly of us, and we want to be respected. But first and foremost, we need to seek God's approval; His opinion is ultimately the only one that matters. His approval allows us to rest securely and safely in His eternal love and His everlasting grace.

Instead of seeking others' approval, Lord, may I strive to know and please You.

Finding Rest in This Season

After you have suffered a little while, the God of all grace, who has called you to his eternal glory in Christ, will himself restore, confirm, strengthen, and establish you.

—1 Peter 5:10 ESV

We all experience different seasons throughout our lives—seasons of joy and celebration, of grief and despair, and of waiting and receiving. Some last for an instant, while others seem to go on forever. You may not be in the season you desire right now, but you can still find rest where you are.

As humans, our instinct is to look toward the future. If you're in a season of suffering or sadness, you're hoping for a season of relief and celebration. But sometimes the Lord asks you to stay in a season—and it feels exhausting. Yet, dear one, He will give you a reprieve.

God's plan, though you may not understand it, is perfectly thought out. There is a reason you're in this place at this time. Rest in the knowledge that the Lord is right there beside you. And He's telling you, "I am in control. Don't be afraid." Rest in Him.

Oh, God, thank You for being with me, both in the heights of joy and in the depths of sadness.

Rest Through Gratitude

The fear of the LORD leads to life; then one rests content, untouched by trouble.

—Proverbs 19:23

We often associate the word *gratitude* with Thanksgiving. While the turkey is passed, we talk about what we're thankful for, and then we eat pumpkin pie. But why not focus on gratitude throughout the year?

Though it may seem trite or childish, counting our blessings is clearly linked with rest. When we count our blessings, we realize how much we *do* have. And by listing the things we're thankful for, we are less apt to focus on what we don't have.

A grateful heart is a heart at rest. It doesn't want more. It doesn't feel the need to show off or compete or work harder; it is content. Can you say that about yourself?

Today, notice the blessings around you. Open your eyes to this wondrous world. You'll find your heart less inclined to covet and envy, and instead, you'll find a peace that passes all understanding. It is the peace of contentment and rest.

Lord, teach me to see the many blessings You bring to me every day.

APRIL

Jesus said to them, "Come with me by yourselves to a quiet place and get some rest."

—Mark 6:31

Committed to Rest

May your hearts be fully committed to the LORD our God, to live by his decrees and obey his commands, as at this time.

—1 Kings 8:61

People often say they're committed to their jobs, family, or faith, but have you ever heard anyone say, "I'm committed to rest"?

Committing to rest is a countercultural goal. We're programmed to go faster, harder, and longer—and rest is too often seen as a weakness. But the Bible commands us to rest, and so it's important that we are committed to rest.

How can you commit to resting? Make conscious choices. Set aside time each day to read Scripture and talk with your Father. Turn off technology and be present with your family. Listen to your body and take a nap if you need one. Hold God's approval over others' opinion of yourself. Take a walk outside. Focus on gratitude. There are many, many ways you can rest, and the act of resting should be specifically tailored to meet your needs. Learn what is most effective for you, and then commit to your own way of resting.

Lord, I commit to resting, physically and spiritually, so that I may be a better witness for You.

Risking Vulnerability

How good and pleasant it is when God's people live together in unity!

—Psalm 133:1

Who do you go to when you have a prayer request? Or you're having a hard day? Or you simply need help? If certain individuals pop into your head, those people are your community. They're the ones who can help you rest in tangible ways—and they're the ones with whom you can risk being vulnerable.

Being vulnerable isn't a comfortable feeling in today's do-it-yourself society. But once you risk being honest and vulnerable with someone, chances are that person will risk being honest and vulnerable with you too.

Perhaps you've just had surgery and need help with meals; ask your community. Maybe you need help with a new baby; ask your community. Or perhaps you're weary of searching for a job; ask your community for prayers. Be brave enough to risk asking for help, to risk being vulnerable. And when you feel rested, be sure to return the favor.

Lord, it's hard to ask for help. Give me the courage to be vulnerable with my community.

Rest in the Morning

*In the morning, LORD, you hear my voice; in the morning I lay my
requests before you and wait expectantly.*

—Psalm 5:3

A two-hour nap may not be a good use of your time today.
A weeklong vacation may not be in the budget. But be
assured, you can still make rest a part of your day.

It may seem counterintuitive to lose sleep, but setting your alarm just twenty minutes earlier could give you
enough time to sip your coffee in peace, pray, and take
some deep breaths before the busyness of your day begins.
Your mind will be more focused, peaceful, and energized
than if you had just rolled out of bed and hit the ground
running. In fact, if you keep up this habit of early morning rest, you'll soon be unable to imagine your mornings
without that quiet time.

Give waking up earlier a try and see what a difference
it makes in your life. By beginning your morning with
intentional rest, you'll be set for a more stress-free and
rest-filled day.

*Father, please bless my times of rest. May I see fruit from my early
morning time with You.*

Rest in the Afternoon

"My hand will sustain him; surely my arm will strengthen him."
—Psalm 89:21

Sometimes the morning flies by, but other times it creeps by with agonizing slowness. Regardless, the afternoon slump always finds you. You crave a nap, you brew another cup of coffee, and you hope to make it until dinner. Sound familiar?

Consider resting in your afternoon. You might not be able to curl up for a nap at work, or even at home, if kids are running around. However, your afternoon slump may be the time that rest is most crucial for you—and rest doesn't always look like sleep.

Find rest by stepping outside for ten minutes. Walk around and breathe in the fresh air. Send the kids to their rooms for some quiet time. Sit on the porch with some tea. Close your office door or slip away to a quiet spot and pray, asking your Father for energy.

If you intentionally rest during your afternoons, you can combat the afternoon crash. Have hope today, because you can find rest.

Father, please revive me and help me find rest—and You—in my afternoons.

Connect with God

Stay focused; listen to the wisdom I have gained; give attention to what I have learned about life.

—Proverbs 5:1 VOICE

Your alarm beeps, and you wake up, automatically reaching to check your e-mail on your phone. You hear a buzzing noise and rummage in your bag for your phone. You need to check the time, so you grab your phone. And the list goes on.

There are so many ways your phone is helpful: it offers the time, directions, information, quick communication, and video chats with faraway family. There are countless apps to help with everything from tracking your daily steps to delivering your favorite pizza. Yet sometimes you just need to disconnect the phone and connect with God.

Disconnecting wasn't a needed concept a few years ago when a phone was nothing more than a phone. But with the invention of smartphones, disconnecting is now a necessity.

Challenge yourself to disconnect today. Sit in silence and prayer. Pay attention to what the Lord is saying to you, and revel in the gift of quiet, disconnected time.

Remind me, Lord, to disconnect from my phone and to connect with You.

Let the World Go By

"I have told you these things, so that in me you may have peace. In this world you will have trouble. But take heart! I have overcome the world."

—John 16:33

You might feel frazzled right now. Your brain is spinning a million miles an hour, and your shoulders are so tense, they're hunched up to your ears. You have so much to do that it feels like a stretch to even sit down and read these words. Sound familiar?

Stop. Just for a few minutes, let the world pass by. Time is ticking—and it is so very valuable—but even more precious is the time you spend in rest with the Lord. Breathe deeply; calm your heart. Relax your shoulders, and let your mind become still.

Right now, in this moment, God wants you to give it all to Him: your busy schedule, your worries about finances, the stress you're feeling at work, the heartbreak you're nursing. He wants you to trust Him, and He wants you to trust that even as the world continues on, you're doing the right thing by resting in Him.

Father, help me step away from this world's busyness and rest in You.

When You Can't Go On

I lift up my eyes to the mountains—where does my help come from?
My help comes from the LORD, the Maker of heaven and earth.

—Psalm 121:1–2

You're exhausted. There's no other way to put it. When you wake up, you want to go back to sleep. And when you fall asleep, the morning comes far too quickly. You survive on coffee and adrenaline, and you crave sleep like a desert wanderer craves water.

Friend, exhaustion *is* real. And this world can be overwhelming. Responsibility is all-consuming, and it may seem as if you'll never get a break. Listen carefully: God does not want you to do it all. He doesn't want you to be so tired that you're barely hanging on to sanity.

Ask God for help today. Ask Him to lead you to someone—a sister, brother, parent, friend, neighbor, colleague, or fellow church member—who can ease your burden. Healing your body, mind, and soul of exhaustion is so much more important than looking as if you have it all together. You don't need to be exhausted any longer; help is on its way.

Jesus, I lift my eyes to You. I am exhausted and weak. Rescue me.

You Can't Force It

I have put my trust in you. Show me the way I should go.

—Psalm 143:8

When you're putting together a puzzle, whether it's a hundred-piece puzzle or a thousand-piece puzzle, one thing remains true: you can't force the pieces together. Even when you think a piece belongs somewhere, if it doesn't fit, it simply won't work. You'll have to move on and find a piece that does fit.

And can't the same be said for our life plans? It can be tempting to force our own plans into action. When we know what we want, and we think we have the right piece of the puzzle for it to work, we might try to force it into place. Then we don't understand why the job doesn't pan out or the relationship doesn't last.

If you're trying to force a puzzle piece to fit and it's not working, ask the Lord to show you the right piece. Rely on His expertise. After all, He's the master Puzzle Maker, and He knows how to take seemingly disconnected pieces and turn them into a beautiful life.

Dear Lord, show me how to put the puzzle of this life together in a way that glorifies You.

Drop Out of the Competition

"The LORD does not look at the things people look at. People look at the outward appearance, but the LORD looks at the heart."

—1 Samuel 16:7

Spring is coming—and with it a flurry of photos on social media. Whether you use Twitter, Instagram, or Facebook, vacation photos will be everywhere. You scroll, scroll, scroll through images of exotic cruises, relaxing beach resorts, peaceful cabin settings, and luxurious island hopping. And though the pictures are beautiful, your heart is not.

Envy creeps in. You want to either criticize your friends' photos—or criticize yourself for not having the picture-perfect vacation. *Stop*—and that's a command said in love.

That picture-perfect life isn't attainable. It's an illusion that keeps us striving and searching. There is only One who will truly satisfy, only One who perfectly measures up to God's standards: Jesus.

Rest in the truth that God doesn't look at your appearance, vacation photos, relationship status, or material wealth; He looks at your heart. And He invites you to rest. So drop out of the social media competition, and find quiet in your own circumstances.

Life is harder when I compare myself to others, God. Turn my eyes to You instead.

Rest in God's Hands

*Wait on the LORD; be of good courage, and He shall strengthen
your heart; wait, I say, on the LORD!*

—Psalm 27:14 NKJV

When events seem out of control, it's easy to feel as if *you*
are spinning out of control. Maybe you've lost your job,
a loved one, or a big portion of your finances. Perhaps your
child just shared some earth-shattering news, or you're not
getting along with your spouse. So many things can make
your life feel out of control, and it's hard not to crumble
along with the mess.

The Lord wants you to look to Him when things are
out of control. When you're knee-deep in bills, heart-
broken with sorrow, or stressed beyond belief, He wants
to hear your troubles. Your life is not really out of control; it is in the hands of a very able and loving Father. Not
only does He know exactly what you need, but He also has
a good, perfect, and redemptive plan for your life. Rest in
knowing that your life is in His hands.

*Lord, I feel so out of control. I need to know that You are in
control.*

Rest from "More" and "Better"

If we have food and clothing, we will be content with that.

—1 Timothy 6:8

Look around any bookstore, and you'll see bestsellers with titles boasting the words *stronger, calmer, richer, thinner, faster,* or *greater.* Our culture tells us we need to be better and have more—according to its standards. We need more success. We need more money. A better life lies in being thinner.

And every year we make resolutions that revolve around "more" and "better." *This will be the year,* we think. We mark the calendar, make a plan, buy a book, find accountability, and then, so often, we fail.

Yes, it's great to be healthier, more organized, more strategic, or more successful. But there's also danger in continually trying to meet the world's standards of "more" and "better." It's all right to sometimes say, "I'm going to rest instead, and I'm going to look for 'more' and 'better' in the Lord." That isn't being lazy; it's being intentional with the time God has given you. Rest from "more" and "better."

Lord, I get so caught up in the race of this world; help me rest from all my striving.

God Will Teach You

"I will instruct you and teach you in the way you should go; I will counsel you with my loving eye on you."

—Psalm 32:8

Read the words of Psalm 32:8 again. How wonderful! What a promise! And what a relief!

Do you worry about what will happen next? Does your heart pound when you look at the future? Are finances, employment, family, love, and the uncertainty of it all weighing on you? If so, Psalm 32:8 is for you.

God promises to teach and instruct you in the way you should go. He will direct your path. And not only will He guide your steps, He'll do it in a loving manner. Does that bring you relief?

You can rest from worrying about the future. The Lord will provide for you. Before you even ask, He knows what you need. Listen to His voice guiding you, and follow the path He lays before you. Leave the future to the Lord.

When I am worried about the future, Lord, whisper Your promises in my ear.

Resisting Recognition

"Your Father, who sees what is done in secret, will reward you."
—Matthew 6:6

Recognition is an enticing word. It feels good to be recognized for our efforts, whether it's as a spouse, parent, friend, colleague, or teacher. We like knowing that we're seen and valued. It can give us a boost of confidence in our abilities, life trajectory, and work. But seeking recognition sometimes leads to sin.

Constantly chasing recognition can leave you tired and frustrated. You worked so hard, but still didn't get that promotion, or an undeserving colleague was named Employee of the Year. You went all out to make a healthy meal, and your kids just complained. You sent that family in need a check, and they never said thank you. You want to be acknowledged. You want to be applauded. You want to be . . . *recognized.*

Rest in this truth: God sees you—as a child, friend, family member, and precious treasure. You are seen, and your efforts are recognized.

God, You are the One I should be adoring. Forgive me for seeking recognition instead of seeking You.

A Haven of Rest

I lie down and sleep; I wake again, because the L<small>ORD</small> sustains me.
—Psalm 3:5

When you look at photos of a resort or retreat center, the bedrooms are serene and calm. They aren't cluttered, and they have crisp, white sheets on a large, luxurious bed, with sunlight filtering through fingerprint-free windows.

When you walk into your own bedroom, does it evoke the same feelings of peace and serenity? Or do you trip over piles of dirty laundry, random stuff, and a few discarded books just to reach your bed? If your bedroom—the place you go to for rest—isn't a haven of peace, it may be time to make a few small changes.

Tidy up, declutter, and freshen up your bedroom. Make it a place where you can breathe in peace—not a place where you look around and see only more things to do. If you make your bedroom a sanctuary and a retreat, your body and mind will be freed to rest. Create your haven—and find rest.

Help me create a haven of rest, Lord, a place to linger in Your presence.

Preparing for the Sabbath

"Say to the Israelites, 'You must observe my Sabbaths. This will be a sign between me and you for the generations to come, so you may know that I am the LORD, who makes you holy.'"

—Exodus 31:13

Have you ever thought about preparing for the Sabbath? It can make a big difference in how your Sabbath feels. If you stay out late the night before, fight with your kids before walking into church, or struggle to stay engaged with the sermon because you're exhausted, your Sabbath won't truly feel like a day of rest. Instead, it can end up feeling like just another day you're trying to get through.

Challenge yourself to cultivate a mind-set of rest before the Sabbath even begins. Commit to going to bed early. Make a list of things that interfere with a true day of rest—whether it's laundry, doing dishes, making meals, doing homework, or other tasks—and commit to resting from them as much as possible on the Sabbath, not out of legalism, but out of a desire for true rest. When God asked us to remember the Sabbath, He meant it. Intentionally seek rest this Sabbath day.

Lord, I want to prepare for the Sabbath more intentionally. Please show me how I can do that this week.

Rest on the Inside

He is our God and we are the people of his pasture, the flock under his care.

—Psalm 95:7

From the outside, your life might look like a whirlwind. Your schedule may be packed and your planner full, but you feel content and at peace; you feel at rest. Or perhaps, from the outside, your life looks completely peaceful. You wake up and work out, your meals are unhurried and nourishing, and you get nine hours of sleep every night. But your soul is not at rest.

Inner rest is even more important than clearing your schedule or slowing your pace of life. It's a posture of humility and grace, and it relies completely on the strength of the living God. Take a close look at your life. Do you have rest within? As you seek inner rest, and as you set aside time to spend soaking in the Lord's presence, you may find your outward life slowly conforming to a pattern of rest too.

My soul longs to be at rest, Father. Restore me to a place of peace.

Sit and Listen

"If my people would only listen to me."

—Psalm 81:13

There are many different ideas of what your time with God should look like. Intensive Bible study with concordances and commentaries, journaling, quiet reflection, a daily devotional, a walk in the woods. Yes, there are countless ways to spend time with the Lord, and one of those is *rest*.

What if you simply sat quietly in His presence and listened? What if you brought nothing to your quiet time except a listening ear and an open heart? It may be a foreign concept to you, and you might even feel as if you're doing something wrong by *not* doing anything. But sometimes we need to sit in the Lord's presence and open our hearts to Him. Allow yourself to find rest in the open arms of a perfect, loving, and holy God; sometimes that's just what you need.

Today, look to your heavenly Father and simply relish knowing that He is with you, for you, and in love with you.

Father, my heart is open and listening to hear Your voice. Thank You for speaking to Your child.

Rest from Complaining

Do everything without grumbling or arguing, so that you may become blameless and pure, "children of God without fault in a warped and crooked generation." Then you will shine among them like stars in the sky.

—Philippians 2:14–15

The grocery lines are too long, the traffic is crazy, and your colleague made a remark that set your blood boiling. Your cereal was soggy, your car is too old, and your mom is driving you nuts. We voice so many complaints every single day. But is it worth it?

Often, complaining puts us in an even lower mood. And after complaining doesn't fix the issue, we complain again. A complaining attitude can affect our friends, family, and fellow workers, as well as anyone who simply crosses our path. Why not rest from complaining?

Every time you start to complain, remind yourself to rest instead. Focus on the positive. Take a deep breath and move on. Send up a prayer for God's protection over your words.

Complaining can be a full-time job, so today take a vacation—a permanent one—from complaining.

Lord, gently remind me to focus on the positive when I am tempted to grumble.

Rest from Procrastination

If anyone, then, knows the good they ought to do and doesn't do it,
it is sin for them.

—James 4:17

You did it again. The clock is ticking and the deadline is approaching. At this rate, you don't know how you're going to get everything finished. But you know how you arrived in this state: you procrastinated. You know that procrastination brings unnecessary stress and exhaustion into your life—so why not make it a goal to eliminate it?

In what areas do you procrastinate? Maybe it's waiting to complete your taxes until the eleventh hour, or planning your anniversary trip the day before. Maybe it's pushing off that work project until the deadline is uncomfortably close, waiting to book plane tickets until prices skyrocket, or saving your shopping until December 24. Sound familiar?

Procrastination is not the answer to a restful life. Free your life of some stress by resting from procrastination. Choose to do this today . . . and not tomorrow.

You know my struggles with procrastination, Lord. Help me kick
this habit out of my life.

What a Friend

"No longer do I call you servants, for the servant does not know what his master is doing; but I have called you friends, for all that I have heard from my Father I have made known to you."

—John 15:15 ESV

There are some friends who just *get* you. When you see one another, even after months or years apart, you simply pick up where you left off. There's no discomfort, no need for small talk, and polite introductions happened a long time ago. Those types of friends are keepers.

Jesus is one of those friends; in fact, He's the perfect Friend. He knows all your sins, insecurities, and embarrassments. And He loves you unconditionally. He sees you fail every single day, and He still wants to spend time with you. Amazing, isn't it?

If you haven't spoken to Jesus in a while, go to Him with confidence. See Him running toward you, eager to welcome you back; feel Him embrace you tenderly; and relax in the realization that He is faithful to you. Jesus' friendship provides rest for our striving, searching, discontented souls. What a Friend we have in Him.

You are the best Friend I've ever had, Jesus. You're always here for me. Thank You.

You Are a Delight

We are God's handiwork, created in Christ Jesus to do good works, which God prepared in advance for us to do.

—Ephesians 2:10

You are an accountant, nurse, firefighter, musician. You are a father, mother, sister, grandparent, friend. You are gentle and loyal, feisty and funny, intelligent and strong. You are so many things wrapped into one body.

You *are* a delight. But you may not feel delightful; you may feel weak, discouraged, overwhelmed, or angry. You might even wish you were a completely different person. Maybe you want to be taller, thinner, richer, or calmer. But guess what? You're you, and there's no one else like you. You're individually made with unique gifts. Your mind, voice, laugh, and personality are wonderfully irreplaceable.

Stop trying to be someone you're not—and start being the person God created you to be: yourself. Rest in that thought today, and every time you begin to criticize yourself, ask your Maker for perspective. Embrace yourself, and find rest in who you are—a beloved child of God.

When I am tempted to be someone I'm not, remind me that I'm Your beloved child.

Acting on Anxiety

When anxiety was great within me, your consolation brought me joy.

—Psalm 94:19

Anxiety is real. It is all-consuming and paralyzing, and it often can make you feel out of control, isolated, and fearful. Maybe you experience it on a daily basis, or perhaps you only have anxiety when you're flying in an airplane or riding in a taxi. Every person has varying degrees of anxiety in life, but the truth is simple: it can overtake you.

If you are feeling anxious today, there is hope. You can find rest from it. And you can overcome it. There will be a day when your heart won't race uncontrollably. There will be a time when you won't feel overwhelmed.

The first step to overcoming anxiety is to take action: ask for help from God, and then seek out a family member, friend, or counselor. Fill your mind with scriptures about God's peace. And find hope knowing that your anxiety will not last forever. You will find rest.

Father, when anxiety threatens to consume me, lead me to Your refuge and calm my troubled heart.

No Guilt in No

"All you need to say is simply 'Yes' or 'No.'"

—Matthew 5:37

Fact: when you say no to one thing, it allows you to say yes to other things that are more important to you.

If you're a people pleaser, it's difficult to say no. You'd rather say yes and overwhelm yourself than say no and disappoint someone else. But when your yeses begin to pile up, they take valuable time away from other aspects of your life: your work, friends, family, church life, *and* your rest. When you say yes, it feels good to help someone out. But sometimes you're hurting yourself in the process.

That's why guilt shouldn't be attached to the word *no*. Saying no isn't selfish or self-centered or greedy; it's simply treating your own time as valuable. Jesus didn't say yes to everyone; He left the crowds, spent time with His disciples, and rested.

If you begin to say yes out of guilt today, stop yourself and ask God if you should—politely, gently, and lovingly—say no.

When I begin to say yes out of guilt, Lord, stop me and remind me of my limits.

Give Your Loved Ones to the Lord

Sovereign LORD, you are God! Your covenant is trustworthy, and you have promised these good things to your servant.

—2 Samuel 7:28

You don't want your dad to fall in his old age. Your friend is continually making bad financial decisions. Your mom lost her job. Your son is being bullied. Your daughter just received a scary diagnosis. Watching loved ones suffer, grow old, make bad choices, or struggle is scary and very difficult. It would be so much easier if you could be in control . . . or would it?

Are you worried about a loved one today? Is it making you anxious or causing you pain? Rest in the Lord's control. He who holds the universe in His hands knows every detail of the situation. He knows the outcome, and He asks you to trust in His timing, provision, and comfort.

It's difficult, but it's also so very freeing to acknowledge that you don't have control. But you do have a God who loves you deeply and fully. He can give you rest, even from your deepest fears and heartaches.

Jesus, I commit everyone I love into Your able, steady, and loving hands.

When Finances Look Bleak

Some trust in chariots and some in horses, but we trust in the name of the LORD our God.

—Psalm 20:7

You swipe your credit card to pay for groceries and inwardly wince. You put your tithe in the offering plate at church and pray the Lord will provide. You try to pick up odd jobs here and there, and you're an expert on coupons. Still, your finances look bleak.

If you're wrestling with money worries, hear these words: God knows your needs. He knows how much those car repairs will cost, how long you'll be unemployed, and when the next tuition payment is due. He's intimately involved in your life, and He cares deeply about you and your well-being.

Take a deep breath and feel the air rush through your lungs. The Lord—who formed your airways and the very oxygen molecules that fill them—knows *everything* you need, and He promises to provide. Cling to His promises today. When your finances look bleak, rest in the provision of the cross.

You promise to provide for me, Lord, and I am choosing to trust Your words.

When Life Isn't as You Had Hoped

But as for me, I watch in hope for the LORD, I wait for God my Savior; my God will hear me.

—Micah 7:7

How did I end up here? you wonder. Life just doesn't look the way you envisioned it when you were younger. It's much harder—more responsibility, sorrow, pain, and stress. Playing house as a child doesn't compare to everyday life as an adult, does it?

When life isn't going the way you'd hoped, it's easy to be discouraged. Maybe you're working a dead-end job, or your dream of being a musician is fading. Your mom died too soon, your spouse left, parenthood is a tough battle, or your close friend betrayed you. Life throws curveballs, and sometimes you get hit.

How do you cope? How can you find rest and contentment? Scripture tells us that our only hope comes from God. Tell Him your struggles, and confide your fears in His ear. He is listening—and waiting to give you rest.

My hope, satisfaction, joy, and future are in You, my God, my Savior, and my King.

Overcome Envy

Envy rots the bones.

—Proverbs 14:30

Envy begins subtly, but then it "rots the bones." And like a weed, once it takes root, it spreads quickly and is hard to kill.

Our materialistic culture pushes the notion of never having enough, and many of us have come to believe this lie. When we see someone else looking happy, we want what they have: a cruise to Aruba, perfect skin, a more impressive job title, a more attractive spouse, better behaved children, a flawless body—the list goes on and on.

Envy is controlling, but it doesn't need to control you. It can be overcome. Find rest from envy, and you'll find contentment and richness in your own life and your own story. Instead of letting envy rot your bones, halt it before it can enter any part of your heart. Ask God to take every thought captive and fill you with gratitude instead—then rest in gratitude for all the Giver has given you.

Please, Lord, take all my thoughts captive—especially the envious ones—and give me rest.

Go Outside

Since the creation of the world God's invisible qualities—his eternal power and divine nature—have been clearly seen, being understood from what has been made, so that people are without excuse.

—Romans 1:20

Many studies have shown that being outdoors is not only good for your physical well-being, it's also good for your mental and social well-being. Nature helps increase attention span, creativity, problem-solving skills, and self-esteem. It can reduce stress, increase conflict resolution skills, strengthen immunity, raise test scores, and ease depression.

With all those benefits, why not go outside? The great outdoors is a great place to unwind and rest. Whether you take a long bike ride, walk along a hiking trail, jog around your neighborhood, or simply sit by the lake, you'll see great benefits to resting intentionally outdoors.

God's creation is beautiful, and it's also restorative, inspiring, and soothing. If you're feeling weary or simply in need of a break from everyday life, open the door and step outside. Rest in the wonders of being in the open air.

When I look at the work of Your hands, Lord, my heart is full of wonder.

A Good Question to Ask

[Make] the best use of the time, because the days are evil. Therefore do not be foolish, but understand what the will of the Lord is.

—Ephesians 5:16–17 ESV

Here's an important question to contemplate: *Is this the best use of my time?*

You may be surprised by how often your answer is no. After eliminating those ten minutes of Internet scrolling, or half hour of stewing over a fight with your spouse, or an hour of mindlessly watching a television show you're only half interested in, you may find that you have more time in your day than you thought.

By asking, *Is this the best use of my time?* you can fill the spaces you have freed up with something life-giving—like taking a nap, spending time in prayer, playing with your child, calling your sister, or reading a good book. Or you could get some of life's necessities out of the way, like packing school lunches, prepping for a conference call, or balancing the budget . . . leaving you with more room for intentional rest.

Lord, remind me that time is fleeting, and guide me to a more intentional, rested life.

Rest in Reconciliation

He will yet fill your mouth with laughter and your lips with shouts of joy.

—Job 8:21

We all have difficult relationships at some point in our lives. Whether it's with our parents, siblings, fellow churchgoers, coworkers, friends, or children, relational turmoil is unavoidable. We are broken people, and we sometimes say and do hurtful things to one another.

Is there a tumultuous relationship in your life? Is it giving you anxiety or keeping you up at night? Do you have a knot in your stomach when you think about that person? If so, tell the Lord about it. Ask Him to reveal truth to your heart and the other person's heart as well.

Navigating broken relationships can be stressful, awkward, and painful. But when you are walking with the Lord, He can lift that burden from you and guide you along His perfect pathway. Ask Him to give you rest from this tough relationship today. And find restful freedom in knowing that He delights in walking alongside His children, even in the most difficult times.

Father, You love reconciliation. Please bring peace to this difficult relationship.

MAY

"*Whoever listens to me will live in safety
and be at ease, without fear of harm.*"

—Proverbs 1:33

When the Answer Isn't Instant

The LORD is my strength and my shield; my heart trusts in him, and he helps me. My heart leaps for joy, and with my song I praise him.
—Psalm 28:7

We live fast-paced lives. We want one-day shipping, five-minute meals, and instant results. Our culture expects instant gratification, so when we have to wait, it can feel excruciating.

Are you waiting for an answer today? Maybe you've been longing for a spouse or a child, but the answer so far seems to be no. Perhaps you're searching for a new job, trying to save for retirement, or waiting for a loved one to return from deployment. We wait in countless ways, and most of the time, our prayers are not instantly answered. And that's okay.

It's okay because God has a plan bigger than your own. He hears your prayers, and He knows your desires. He isn't ignoring you; He's simply working in His way and in His time. Rest in the knowledge that God is good and loving, and He loves to give you good gifts—they just aren't often overnighted.

Help me trust that You want only good things for me, Lord— especially while I am waiting.

Rest from Outward Perfection

Your beauty should not come from outward adornment, such as elaborate hairstyles and the wearing of gold jewelry or fine clothes. Rather, it should be that of your inner self, the unfading beauty of a gentle and quiet spirit, which is of great worth in God's sight.

—1 Peter 3:3–4

Are you striving to appear a certain way? Do you want others to think you're supermom or superdad, a powerful CEO, a woman who can do it all, a man who is the life of the party, or the church member with the perfect family? Those certainly aren't bad things, but is your striving taking over your life? Are you too busy worrying about *how you look* to find time to actually rest and be content with *who you are*?

The truth is, we all fall short. We all make mistakes and let others down. No one has it all together. And though we try to appear perfect, in fact, we are far from it.

The Bible says people look at the outward appearance, but the Lord looks at the heart (1 Samuel 16:7). Instead of running after a perfect appearance, ask God to transform your heart and to give you rest from pursuing an outer image that will never truly satisfy.

Heavenly Father, transform my heart. Renew a right spirit within me and cleanse my soul from sin.

Look Up

"Blessed are those who trust in the LORD and have made the LORD their hope and confidence."

—Jeremiah 17:7 NLT

When your alarm clock begins blaring, the baby wakes up, or your meeting gets moved up to 7 a.m., it's all too easy to begin your day in a rush. But consider this: beginning with rest can transform your entire day.

It is often in the quiet and stillness that we hear God's voice. When we look to Him first thing in the morning, we acknowledge that we cannot get through this day on our own strength. When we surrender the day and all its frustrations, joys, and stresses to Him, we can rest, knowing He is in control.

Begin your day looking up at the Lord instead of looking at your own two feeble hands. Even if you only have a brief moment on one of "those" mornings, breathe in His peace, His presence, and His provision. Be relieved of the burden of control. Rest in knowing that the Lord walks with you.

Bless me this morning, God, and remind me of Your presence throughout my day today.

Rest Through Trust

Teach me knowledge and good judgment, for I trust your commands.

—Psalm 119:66

When you are in the presence of someone you don't trust, how do you act? Your guard is probably up, while your mind sifts through that person's intentions, actions, and words. You are on high alert.

But when you're with someone you trust, your demeanor is completely different. You're relaxed. Your words spill out comfortably, and you breathe deeply and laugh with ease. You feel at rest. Trust is a game changer.

When you trust the Lord with your plans, fears, hopes, and aspirations, you can relax. You can rest. He is more trustworthy than anyone in the universe, and you can rest assured that He wants only the very best for you. Trust isn't a blind free-fall into the Lord's arms; it's a bold and confident leap that comes from knowing He's been faithful to His people for thousands of years. Trust Him and His good plans today. Let Him give you rest.

I trust and adore You, my Father and King. I rest in Your presence.

A Sweet Rest

Nehemiah said, "Go and enjoy choice food and sweet drinks, and send some to those who have nothing prepared. This day is holy to our Lord. Do not grieve, for the joy of the LORD is your strength."
—Nehemiah 8:10

In Sweden, colleagues, friends, or family gather during the workday for a break called *fika*. It takes place each morning and afternoon, and it's accompanied by coffee, a sweet treat, and company. It's a cultural norm, and it would be considered abnormal not to partake in *fika*. Can you imagine what your life would be like with an intentional *fika*?

Whether at work or home, with family, colleagues, or a new friend, *fika* is used to enjoy quality time with others. It's a well-deserved break from the daily grind. *Fika* intentionally carves out time to slow down, take a break, and decompress.

What would it take to institute *fika* in your own life? It may take some planning and discussing, but intentional rest can happen, even in the busiest of lives. Find time today to enjoy *fika*, and savor sweet rest.

I need Your help to put intentional rest into my days, Lord. Bless me with Your sweet presence!

When the World Feels Brutal

After his suffering, [Jesus] presented himself to them and gave many convincing proofs that he was alive. He appeared to them over a period of forty days and spoke about the kingdom of God.

—Acts 1:3

If you watch the news for five minutes, listen to talk radio, or glance at the newspaper, you'll know our world is extremely broken. Violence, war, injustice, racism, poverty, and more are all still very much alive today—and some days it seems the world is just getting worse and worse.

Take heart; when the world feels brutal and overwhelmingly broken, God is still working. When the headlines cut through your soul and the most recent news makes your breath catch, find courage, because God's love and redemption *will* prevail in the end.

Today, our world is full of suffering. But suffering doesn't get the last word. The almighty God gets the last word—and He promises rest, restoration, and healing. Cling to that knowledge today, and rest in the enduring promises of a very big, very powerful, very loving God.

When the world feels absolutely brutal and broken, may I see glimpses of Your love and grace, Jesus.

Monday's Joy

You have made known to me the paths of life; you will fill me with joy in your presence.

—Acts 2:28

Is it the beginning of the week already? How did the weekend rush by so quickly? You try to lift your spirits for another week, but you're just too tired. You just want one more day of rest, but Monday is already here. Sound familiar?

You can't turn back time, and you can't add one more hour to the weekend, but it is still possible to set a restful tone for the week. How? With joy.

Joy begins with gratitude, and, yes, you *can* find something to be grateful for every single day. It might take practice, but as you search for things to be grateful for, joy will take root in your heart. And that deep joy—the kind that keeps you going despite life's hurdles—will sustain you.

God is just waiting to pour His joy into you. Ask Him to give you a grateful heart and a soul-resting attitude of joy as you begin this week.

Lord, may I go throughout this day with deep gratitude for another chance to live for You.

Falling Down and Getting Up

*Out of his fullness we have all received grace in place of grace
already given.*

—John 1:16

You messed up. You lost your temper. You crossed the line. You chose evil over good. You hurt your friend. Do any of these statements ring true in your life today?

As humans, we fall over and over again. We shake our heads at our mistakes, feel shame, beat ourselves up, and disappoint many. We fall into temptation's trap, act unjustly, and let sin rule our minds. But still, there is grace—grace upon grace upon grace—and the very real assurance of God's never-ending grace is like a deep well of water for a thirsty soul.

God knows we are sinners. He knows our shortcomings and struggles. He knows about that sin you just can't seem to break free from, and He offers you grace. It doesn't make sense, and it isn't contingent on anything you do; instead, it's a reflection of God's goodness and mercy. Dear friend, rest assured: there is grace enough for you.

I don't deserve Your grace, yet You lavish it upon me over and over again. Thank You, Lord.

God Can Handle the Truth

"If my people, who are called by my name, will humble themselves and pray and seek my face and turn from their wicked ways, then I will hear from heaven, and I will forgive their sin and will heal their land."

—2 Chronicles 7:14

Have you ever done anything shameful? Are there sins you're embarrassed to tell even your closest confidant? Do you find yourself hiding from God because your failures are too shocking? Dear one, God can handle the truth.

He asks for obedience, but He welcomes the sinner. He knows no sin, but He loves those who are bound by it. God knows the darkest, most appalling parts of you, and if you confess them to Him, He will not turn you away. Instead, He will wash you clean.

If you're running from the Lord or trying to hide your mistakes, pause, take a deep breath, and turn to Him. Know that there is nothing you can do that is beyond His forgiveness. And there is no way He can love you more or love you less. God can handle the truth, and He longs for you to stop running and, instead, rest in His healing presence.

Here I am, Lord, broken and sinful; thank You for loving me and covering me with Your grace.

You Are Not Forsaken

Those who know your name trust in you, for you, LORD, have never forsaken those who seek you.

—Psalm 9:10

In your darkest moments, you may feel forsaken by God. You might feel that your prayers are falling on deaf ears, or perhaps you think God simply doesn't care about you anymore. Have you ever felt forsaken?

Dear friend, you are not forsaken—and you will never be forgotten. You may be in a dark valley, and your prayers may look as if they've not been answered, but even in the darkness, the Lord is by your side.

Cast away fear and unrest, raise your hands to your heavenly Father, and ask Him to make Himself known to you. He clearly says in His Word that He does not forsake those who seek Him; may you fully understand that truth. The Lord has not forgotten you; He is not ignoring you or turning a deaf ear to your cries. Rest in His arms—He is a loving, faithful, and always present God. Hallelujah!

When I feel forgotten, may I remember Your promise to never leave or forsake me, Father God.

The Struggle to Rest

"You may ask me for anything in my name, and I will do it."

—John 14:14

Rest *is* a struggle. It's not that you don't want to rest, but it can sometimes be so difficult to find space and time to rest well. Sometimes even finding five minutes of alone time is a rare treat, especially if you're a busy student, parent, caregiver, or career-minded individual.

Today, think about what keeps you from rest. Is it the baby who wakes up every three hours? Is it your job, which demands late nights and weekends? Or is it simply an overfilled schedule? Ask the Lord to open up opportunities for rest.

Perhaps He'll remind you to call a friend to babysit for an hour or to set aside one night a week to not answer work calls. Maybe there's a weekly or monthly obligation that you can say no to for a while.

Continue to seek the Lord and to seek rest—He *will* open a door for you.

I am in desperate need of rest, Lord. Please open a door of rest for me soon.

When Work Works Against You

The best-equipped army cannot save a king, nor is great strength enough to save a warrior.

—Psalm 33:16 NLT

A strong work ethic is a great quality to have. It means you work hard and well, and you can be counted on to get the job done. But sometimes a strong work ethic can actually work against you, such as when you begin working night and day, skipping meals, and getting too little sleep because you want to do your job well.

God calls us to work hard. He wants us to work to the best of our ability and to honor and glorify His name through our efforts. But He doesn't want to see us burned out, struggling to stay awake, and becoming resentful of our jobs.

Does your work ethic work against you? Admit that you can't do it all—because you weren't created to do it all. Then treat yourself to some rest. Take a Sabbath; go on a weekend trip. God worked, and then He rested. Take some time to follow His example.

I admit that I can't do it all, Lord. Rescue me with Your rest.

A Snow Day in Spring

Then my soul will rejoice in the LORD and delight in his salvation.

—Psalm 35:9

If you live in a state that gets snow in the winter, you know how exciting snow days are to children (and teachers too). As big flakes fly past the windows, the excitement of a snow day is barely containable. Why do children love snow days so much? They're a chance to sleep in, skip school, and simply enjoy the surprise of a day off.

But you don't have to wait for winter to take a snow day of rest. Any break from your regular routine can be a delightful reprieve.

Every person in every season of life needs a day of rest. It may not look like napping away the afternoon, and it might not happen on Saturday or Sunday. But it does mean you have a chance to sit quietly with the Lord, to let Him feed your soul with His Spirit, and to find rest from this weary world.

Slow me down, Lord. Come into my day, refresh my spirit, and surprise me with rest.

Start Anew

Weeping may stay for the night, but rejoicing comes in the morning.
—Psalm 30:5

Think back just a few months to the beginning of the year. Those early days held expectation and the promise of new hope, a clean slate, and a fresh start. Now you're well into spring—is that anticipation and hopefulness still there? Or do you feel as if you're floundering underwater with no time to come up for air? Perhaps you've thrown up your hands in despair, thinking, *It's just going to be another one of those years*.

Rest assured: there is always room for a new beginning. Yes, life has disappointments—and we often disappoint ourselves—but we're always invited to begin anew.

Even if your year is turning out nothing like you'd wanted or planned, there is hope. Stop beating yourself up. You can begin anew today . . . and tomorrow . . . and the day after that. There is rest after failure, and this time, you can soar.

Father God, remind me that I can always begin anew with You.

If You Step Away . . .

As God's chosen people, holy and dearly loved, clothe yourselves
with compassion, kindness, humility, gentleness and patience.

—Colossians 3:12

If I am not there, everything will fall apart. Many people feel this way about their responsibilities, whether they're a stay-at-home mom, an executive assistant, the president of a nonprofit, or a committed volunteer at the mission.

It's true: things may become a little chaotic if you aren't there. You might come back to more work, a frazzled spouse, or a little disarray. But you might not. And either way, life will go on—even without you there to guide, lead, prod, and pick up the slack.

If you are holding out on rest because you feel you're indispensible, you may want to reconsider. Give someone else a chance to step up, practice responsibility, and increase his or her confidence—and allow yourself some much-needed rest. Take a step back and let things go for a day or even just a few hours. Life will go on, and you'll come back feeling more equipped, capable, and energetic.

Lord, help me remember that the world won't fall apart if I take
time away to rest.

Finding Balance

Commit your way to the Lord; trust in him and he will do this.

—Psalm 37:5

We all crave balance, don't we? There's a cultural obsession with finding the perfect balance of work, rest, family, hobbies, and friends. We want it all, but too often we get caught up in the web of trying to have it all and have it all right now. To put it mildly, finding balance is really hard—and we fail at it all the time.

When you feel as if you can't figure it out, and the puzzle of balance just has too many pieces, turn to the Lord. He's the master Problem Solver. He knows exactly what you need, and He knows how to help you achieve that elusive balance in your life.

Breathe easier, knowing that God is the ultimate Provider of rest, work, and community. He knows these are all good things, and He knows that you sometimes need help balancing them all. Ask God for help, and then wait patiently for His answer.

I'm so relieved, Lord, that You are the master Problem Solver—and that it's not all up to me.

Holy Rest

"The Son of Man is Lord of the Sabbath."

—Matthew 12:8

When you look at the Ten Commandments, notice which commandment God spends the most time on. It isn't murder, stealing, or committing adultery. It's not the commandment to honor your parents or forsake idols. Rather, the longest commandment is to rest.

Do you think there's a reason behind that?

Perhaps it's because God knew that our tendency to lead increasingly busy lives would become harder and harder to free ourselves from—and He was already addressing it thousands of years ago.

When God commands us to rest, it's not because it's good for Him; God tells us to rest because it's good for us. Our bodies were not made to work seven days a week. We are not able to go and go and go like machines; we are human beings, and we are weak.

Remember the Sabbath today, and relax in holy rest.

Lord of the Sabbath, help me remember to rest and to keep Your day holy.

The Top of the List

Restore us, LORD God Almighty; make your face shine on us, that we may be saved.

—Psalm 80:19

Whether you work in an office as a CEO or are a university student, you probably have a few things to do. And some tasks are more pressing than others. That deadline is crucial; your final exam is important; meeting the needs of three hungry kids is a must. There are many priorities in your life, but how can you prioritize rest?

Rest gets pushed aside. You sacrifice sleep—and it's often for good things. You choose a date night over going to bed early. You prepare for a work presentation instead of sleeping in. You cuddle a sick baby and skip a nap of your own. But how often can you sacrifice rest before you are running ragged?

Today, try to prioritize rest in some way. Bump it closer to the top of your list. You'll feel more refreshed, positive, and loving; and those around you will benefit too.

Lord, I often push rest completely off my to-do list. Please show me opportunities to rest today.

Tuning Out the Noise

Then a great and powerful wind tore the mountains apart and shattered the rocks before the LORD, but the LORD was not in the wind.

—1 Kings 19:11

Is your television always on, or is your phone constantly begging for your attention? Do you numb your pain or shut down your thoughts by watching lots of movies? Must the radio always be on when you're driving? Our worlds are often noisy, and though it may feel uncomfortable, we need to seek out a still, peaceful place in order to hear God.

When do you seek rest from noise? Do you look for it in the early morning hours when the moon is fading away, or is it in the evening when the stars are quietly shining? Maybe you protect a few minutes of your afternoon for sitting outside to think, or you take time after dinner to walk and talk with the Lord.

There will always be noise and something vying for your attention. Be sure to intentionally set aside time to rest in the stillness and to listen for the still, small, and pure voice of God.

I am bombarded by the loud demands of this world, Lord. Remind me to listen for Your still, small voice.

Caring for Yourself

*I pray that from his glorious, unlimited resources he will empower
you with inner strength through his Spirit.*

—Ephesians 3:16 NLT

Imagine yourself with a sweet child. But instead of treating that child with love and gentleness, you place high demands on her. You wake her after only a few hours of sleep, you make her scrub the floors without breakfast, and you allow her to eat only as you're rushing out the door. After school, you hand her an impossible to-do list—and when dinnertime comes and she hasn't completed it, you yell. You keep her up way past her bedtime and make her feel ashamed when she falls asleep on the couch. Who would treat a child that way?

But . . . is that the way you treat yourself?

Self-care is essential for living a healthy life, and it is also so easy to neglect. Treat yourself like a child today: relax your expectations, be kind to yourself, and rest when you get overwhelmed. Care for yourself.

*Lord, help me tend to my own physical, spiritual, and emotional
needs as a parent tends to a child.*

Resting in Your Purpose

Our purpose is to please God, not people. He alone examines the motives of our hearts.

—1 Thessalonians 2:4 NLT

Why am I here? We all ask this question at some point in our lives. What is our purpose in life? Why did the Lord place each of us, individually, on this earth?

It's tempting to view your career as your purpose. Maybe you're a firefighter or a lawyer, a teacher or a speaker, a stay-at-home mom or dad. All of these are commendable and even needed, but your career isn't your primary purpose for being on earth.

Your role as a grandfather, mother, sister, brother, friend, or aunt isn't your greatest purpose either. What is your greatest purpose? To love the Lord and honor Him with your life.

Find rest and freedom in that today. You are enough—whether you have your dream job or a job that just pays the rent, whether you're single or married, whether you're the parent of a puppy or of ten children—you are enough. Love the Lord, and find rest in fulfilling your greatest purpose today.

Give me freedom in knowing my purpose in this life is to love and honor You, Father.

Rest with Intention

Jesus withdrew again to the mountain by himself.

—John 6:15 ESV

When you finally have a chance to rest, do you actually rest? Or do you fill up your free time with mindless activities such as scrolling through Instagram and refreshing your Facebook feed? When time opens up, do you see that as a chance to rest, or a chance to check something off the to-do list, like shopping, cleaning, or taking on extra work?

Instead of letting precious time for yourself slip away, be intentional with it. Sit with the Lord, journal, and let your mind relax. Do something that fills you with joy, like hiking or gardening. Times of rest need to be enjoyed, and it's only through letting yourself intentionally rest that you will feel refreshed.

Ask God for help in using your times of rest wisely. Sometimes maybe you do simply need to order pizza and watch TV. Or maybe cleaning really does de-stress and relax you. Just be sure that you are intentional during times of rest.

You gave me many examples of how to rest intentionally, Jesus. May I follow Your lead.

Lean on a Friend

Perfume and incense bring joy to the heart, and the pleasantness of a friend springs from their heartfelt advice.

—Proverbs 27:9

"Lean on Me," the song released in 1972, is a good reminder to all of us: we can lean on our friends when we're not strong; we need to give up our pride and ask for help; and we all need someone to lean on.

How often do you lean on your friends? If you need an hour to yourself, do you call a friend to watch your children? When you are behind on your big work project, do you ask your friends for prayers? In times when you're beyond exhausted, do you confide in your friends?

Our friends help us carry on. They care for us and want to help us, whether it's with action, prayer, or simply a listening ear. When you're weary, call on a friend. Admit that you can't do everything on your own, and your friend will be there in a flash, saying, "Lean on me."

I praise You, Lord, for putting friends in my life to lean on when I'm in need.

Sit Still

The eyes of the LORD are everywhere, keeping watch on the wicked and the good

—Proverbs 15:3

As you read these words, do you feel the urge to get up and do something? Are you comfortable sitting still, or do you feel a bit of guilt about even taking time to read this?

We all need time to simply be still, so let yourself sit. God desires to speak to you, and He often speaks loudest when you push away distractions, stop working, and open your ears to what He has to say. Sitting still may feel lazy or unnatural; it may take everything you have not to scroll through your phone or check your e-mail. But being in the Lord's presence may actually be the most productive part of your whole day.

Start your morning with the Giver of life. Let Him carry you and speak to you. Your mind-set and attitude are changed in the presence of the holy God—and all you need to do is be still and listen.

My ears are open, my body is still, and my spirit is ready. Speak to Me, precious Jesus.

Creatures of Discontent

I was young and now I am old, yet I have never seen the righteous forsaken or their children begging bread.

—Psalm 37:25

If you find yourself struggling to be content, it's not surprising. We are bombarded with messages that we don't have enough. Advertisers tell us the happiest people have the newest car, latest phone, biggest wardrobe, and largest bank account. We are discontented creatures, and it all began with Adam and Eve.

When Satan appeared to Adam and Eve and said they could have even more—they could be like God—they wanted it. They saw one thing they didn't have, they set their sights on it, and they sinned. Discontentment prompted the first sin, and we sometimes feel as if it cannot be overcome. But take heart: God *can* bring contentment to your heart.

Are you tired of striving for more? Find rest for your soul by turning to the Lord. When you feel discontentedness creeping in, ask God to show you true fulfillment in Him.

I think I know what I need, Lord, but You truly know what I need. Show me Your fulfillment.

Rest and Eat

He made him ride on the heights of the land and fed him with the fruit of the fields. He nourished him with honey from the rock, and with oil from the flinty crag.

—Deuteronomy 32:13

Rest for your soul is crucial, but rest and care for your body is important too. Did you know that Jesus made sure His disciples took time to rest and eat?

Mark 6:31 says, "Because so many people were coming and going that they did not even have a chance to eat, [Jesus] said to them, 'Come with me by yourselves to a quiet place and get some rest.'"

Jesus knew His disciples hadn't had a chance to eat, and instead of asking them to push through their hunger because their work was too important, He said to walk away from the crowds and eat.

Does this encourage you today? Jesus Himself told His disciples to pause in their ministering, to seek out a quiet place, to rest, and to nourish their bodies. How beautiful! The Lord wants to take care of you spiritually *and* physically. Find time to sit in a quiet place, rest, and eat something healthy today.

Lord, remind me to rest and eat, just as You did for the disciples so many years ago.

Fear of Rest

"Be strong and very courageous. Be careful to obey all the law my servant Moses gave you; do not turn from it to the right or to the left, that you may be successful wherever you go."

—Joshua 1:7

Sometimes we don't rest because we don't have time. But there are other reasons we don't rest, and one may surprise you: fear. We are afraid to rest.

Do you have enough courage to carve out time from your schedule to rest? Or are you worried your boss will perceive you as lazy, or your spouse will be critical of you? Perhaps you feel as if the sky will fall if you step away for a moment, or maybe you don't like feeling unproductive.

You may have fears you need to work through, but fear shouldn't be the reason you're exhausted. It shouldn't be the reason you're working hard, putting in long hours, or staying up all night. Don't allow fear to drive you away from rest. God's perfect love can cast out your fear (1 John 4:8). Hold to that truth as you walk toward the sweet gift of rest.

Be strong and courageous . . . and dare to rest.

Lord, grant me the courage and strength to rest in Your love, letting go of my fears.

Reconnect with the Lord

Whoever gives thought to the word will discover good, and blessed is he who trusts in the Lord.

—Proverbs 16:20 ESV

If you have a close friend who lives a long distance away, you know how wonderful it is when you're together. You may have to board an airplane or train, rent a car, or take the bus, but reconnecting with a friend is worth it. You won't let anything get in the way of meeting with your friend.

When you're finally together, you soak up every single second. You don't spend time worrying about what's going on back home, you don't waste hours on social media, and you make an effort to truly live in the moment.

Your time with the Father can be the same. Even if you haven't connected with Him in a while, He is waiting eagerly for you, and He wants you to fiercely protect your time together with Him. Reconnect with the Lord today, and rejoice that He is always available and never far away.

Lord, I miss being close to You. Help me rest in Your compassionate embrace.

Leave It at the Cross

"He himself bore our sins" in his body on the cross, so that we might die to sins and live for righteousness; "by his wounds you have been healed."

—1 Peter 2:24

What's weighing heavily on your mind today? Is it the sin that so easily entangles you? Are you waiting for the doctor to reveal test results? Are you worried about your son or daughter, your parents or spouse? Do you feel as if you're in over your head? Maybe you feel unloved and unwanted. Whatever it is, it's not too heavy for the cross.

Write down your burdens today—all of them. Whether you're worried about your sickly dog, the paper you need to write, the continual car repairs, or your grandmother's cancer, write it down. Then picture yourself bringing this list of burdens and worries to the cross and leaving it there.

Jesus will take that list from you. He *wants* to carry your burdens for you. He wants to relieve you of the fears you're holding on to and the shame you may be feeling. He wants you to leave everything at the cross and find rest.

Father, thank You for bearing my burdens. Remind me to leave them with You.

Delight in Today

*Who among the gods is like you, LORD? Who is like you—majestic
in holiness, awesome in glory, working wonders?*

—Exodus 15:11

Do you ever just have a bad day? Maybe it began with over-sleeping, or you didn't sleep well and woke up more tired than when you went to bed. Maybe the sky was gray, your children were fighting, and you burned breakfast. Or maybe you just woke up on the wrong side of the bed.

It's okay to admit that some days are hard. But even on the hardest days, you can still be on the lookout for the wonder of God. And the delight you're able to capture has the ability to bring a ray of sunshine to your weary soul and create a bright spot in an otherwise exhausting day.

Wonder can be found in unexpected places. Open your eyes and look for it. Even if your day began in the most difficult of ways, the Lord will bless you with glimpses of His wonder—and with a wonder-filled day.

Lord, when my day gets off on the wrong foot, open my eyes to the wonder of You.

Live Simply

Make it your ambition to lead a quiet life: You should mind your own business and work with your hands, just as we told you.

—1 Thessalonians 4:11

Have you noticed that while laundry detergent used to be limited to a few different types, there are now hundreds of brands boasting fresher scents, whiter whites, fewer chemicals, and more power? And they come in liquids, powders, and pods. Have you ever stood in front of a basic grocery item in the store—from crackers to shampoo—and been utterly overwhelmed by the options?

In today's world, we love options. Whether we're searching for cheap prices or products that are locally made, ethically sourced, or organic, we can have our pick. But do you ever wish the options were a bit more limited?

It may seem like a small, silly thing, but consider limiting your options. Give yourself two options for dinner—tacos or spaghetti; decide between two types of soap or three different selections of thank-you cards. By reducing your choices, you'll save time, energy, and brain space—and you'll open yourself up to rest.

Lord, teach me how to live more simply today.

JUNE

He makes me lie down in green pastures,

he leads me beside quiet waters,

he refreshes my soul.

—Psalm 23:2–3

Rest as a Weapon

The weapons we fight with are not the weapons of the world. On the contrary, they have divine power to demolish strongholds.

—2 Corinthians 10:4

When we think of weapons, we often think of a gun, knife, sword, or bow and arrow. And when we are in danger, we want to be protected—and preferably by someone strong, quick, and capable of taking out the enemy. But have you ever thought of rest as a weapon? It can be.

Rest isn't a weapon we can hold. It doesn't feel particularly strong; in fact, it sounds like something that would make us more vulnerable. After all, how can we protect ourselves if we're at ease? Even though it sounds strange, rest is one of the best weapons in our arsenal.

Rest clears our minds and energizes our bodies, it protects us from sickness, and it makes us think more clearly and love more deeply. Rest protects us mentally, physically, emotionally, and even spiritually.

It may not be as flashy as a sword or a knight in armor, but rest is truly one of our greatest weapons. Arm yourself today.

Lord, when I feel weary and unprotected, remind me to use the weapon of rest.

Set Yourself Free

Return to your rest, my soul, for the LORD has been good to you.
—Psalm 116:7

When you take time out to rest, do you truly free your mind of responsibilities? It's tempting to keep holding on to your responsibilities even as you try to rest. And the truth is, you probably won't rest well if your mind is wrapped around a million other concerns.

Resting isn't passive; it is active. It's an intentional act of slowing down and looking to the Lord for strength. Remember: you can't just fall into rest; you must seek it out.

While resting—whether you're reading your Bible, praying, or sitting in the presence of the Lord—give yourself permission to set your mind free. Give all of your duties, obligations, and stresses to God; He can handle them. Focus on breathing and clearing your mind instead. And every time a worry flutters through your thoughts, surrender it to the Lord.

Jesus, please free my mind of distractions and worries, and help me focus on You.

Restful Hobbies

I said to myself, "Relax and rest. GOD has showered you with blessings. Soul, you've been rescued from death; Eye, you've been rescued from tears; And you, Foot, were kept from stumbling."
—Psalm 116:7–8 THE MESSAGE

Taking on a hobby is a great way to calm your mind. When your brain feels as if it's stuck in overdrive, and your life feels too stressful to handle, you may want to step back, take a break, and immerse yourself in a restful hobby.

Gardening, listening to music, baking, biking, and cooking are all rewarding stress relievers. Reading, fishing, writing, knitting, golfing, and hiking are a few more examples of mind-calming activities.

God created each of us with talents and interests, and we each can find hobbies we enjoy. If you're feeling stressed, turn to a relaxing hobby this week. You don't have to be great at it—the act of going fishing may be just as rewarding as actually catching a bass, and taking a bike ride can be more rejuvenating than participating in a race. The goal isn't to excel; the goal is to relax and enjoy yourself—even if you burn the brownies.

Thank You for making rest enjoyable, Lord. Remind me to take time to do the things I love.

Invest in Rest

Put your ear to the ground and listen, give me space for salvation.
Be a guest room where I can retreat; you said your door was always
open! You're my salvation—my vast, granite fortress.

—Psalm 71:2–3 THE MESSAGE

If you invest your money, you may be pleasantly surprised to find your $100 turned into $1,000 . . . or even more. When you invest in a house, it's always a rewarding feeling to see its value increase. And investing in a friendship can yield one of life's greatest treasures. Investing is a smart thing to do.

But have you considered *retreat* as an investment? If you slipped away from your family to spend one night in solitude, would you feel guilty? If you were to take a day off work due to exhaustion, would you feel ashamed? Friend, rest is an investment in living a healthy life.

When you retreat—whether for a few hours or an entire week—you are actually blessing others. How? Because you return with a renewed outlook, better attitude, and more patience and gentleness. Do you need to invest in rest today?

Remind me that rest is an investment, Lord, and when rested, I'll
bless others more fully.

Don't Wait Until It's Too Late

You will sleep without fear and be greatly respected.

—Job 11:19 CEV

The physical effects of not getting enough sleep include impaired memory, increased blood pressure, increased risk of heart troubles, a weakened immune system, greater susceptibility to illness, weight gain, and type 2 diabetes— and that's just the tip of the iceberg!

That list is scary, but it's also accurate. When we push ourselves to the max, relying on coffee and carbs to get us through the day, we aren't doing ourselves any favors. And too often, we wait until it's too late to rest. By then, our family is frustrated, our work is suffering, and our body is breaking down.

Don't wait until it's too late to rest. Be sure to get adequate sleep, ask friends to keep you accountable, and talk to the Lord about your worries. If you feel as if you simply can't rest, look to the One who watches over you. Ask Him to quiet your soul and lead you to rest.

Lord, I praise You because I am fearfully and wonderfully made. Help me take care of me.

Mary and Martha

"Martha, Martha," the Lord answered, "you are worried and upset about many things, but few things are needed—or indeed only one. Mary has chosen what is better, and it will not be taken away from her."

—Luke 10:41–42

Looking at a massive to-do list with every item checked off can give us a real boost. After all, we all like knowing we've accomplished many tasks throughout the day. We thrive on getting things done and being productive. But . . . is it always healthy?

The Bible doesn't command us to live and die by our to-do lists; God doesn't look at our productivity to decide if we're fit for heaven. When Jesus visited Martha and Mary, He gently scolded Martha for her busyness, telling her that her sister had made the better choice by simply sitting at His feet. Jesus didn't praise Martha for being busy; He used her resting sister, Mary, as an example of what was right.

You may not accomplish everything you set out to do today. But if you intentionally choose to spend time with the Lord, you are following the example of Mary. And you will have "chosen what is better."

Jesus, it's easy for me to be Martha; teach me to take time to be more like Mary.

Rest for Troubled Hearts

When Jesus saw her weeping, and the Jews who had come along
with her also weeping, he was deeply moved in spirit and troubled.

—John 11:33

Do you feel troubled today? Is your heart heavy? Are anxieties and heartache weighing you down? Do you feel burdened? Jesus knows, and He understands. Jesus Himself was troubled by the sin He saw; His Spirit was grieved when Judas betrayed Him; His heart was broken when His friend Lazarus died; and He carried the greatest of all burdens—the cross. Yes, Jesus understands all about troubled hearts.

And because Jesus understands, we have hope. For although the Lord suffered and died, He also rose victorious from the grave. Jesus took the burden of the cross so that we don't have to. His death wiped away our sins, rendering them forgiven and forgotten. And His resurrection conquered death and offers the promise of life eternal.

The story of Jesus is the story of redemption. He gives strength and rest to the weary; He gives life, hope, and joy to troubled hearts. Rest in Jesus' victory today.

You understand suffering and grief, Jesus. Please grant me rest for
my troubled soul.

Overcoming Disappointment

I come to you for shelter. Protect me, keep me safe, and don't
disappoint me.

—Psalm 25:20 CEV

We have all experienced disappointment. In games, there's always a loser. In a job interview, only one person is hired. When a relationship fizzles, a dream is dashed, or another person gets what you so desperately wanted, it's incredibly painful and disappointing. If we're not careful, disappointment can lead to despair, and despair only brings misery and discontent.

When you're disappointed, moving on can be tough. Wallowing and moping are much easier. But if you linger in the muck of disappointment, you'll constantly be fighting to keep your head above the water—which is completely exhausting.

Be encouraged. The Lord knows how it feels to be disappointed, and He wants to free you from its chains. Because of His power and love, you don't need to be consumed by disappointment; instead, you can move on with His joy and hope as your guide. Flee from disappointment and run straight into His waiting arms.

When I am disappointed, Lord, remind me that Your hope never
disappoints.

Resting from the Love of Money

The love of money causes all kinds of trouble. Some people want money so much that they have given up their faith and caused themselves a lot of pain.

—1 Timothy 6:10 CEV

There's a reason the lottery rakes in more than $70 billion each year—because many believe that money brings happiness. If your bank account is overflowing, material desires are all met, and nothing is out of your price range, then surely you'll feel satisfied, right?

Money, in some ways, does make life easier. You can pay the bills without feeling stressed. But once your physical needs are met, happiness doesn't necessarily increase in proportion to the size of your checking account. Riches can certainly appear tantalizing and even fun, but in the end, only Jesus can truly satisfy.

If the desire for more money is plaguing you, ask God to help you desire more of Him instead. Find rest in His promises to take care of all your needs—and enjoy the amazing riches of a life lived *for* and *with* and *in* Him.

Father, please change my desire for money into an unquenchable desire for You.

God's Love Isn't Earned

So the promise is received by faith. It is given as a free gift.
—Romans 4:16 NLT

God's love cannot be earned. If you give up all your possessions, move to a third-world country, and serve the most unlovable of people, you will not be given a greater portion of God's love. If you volunteer for every church need, evangelize on the weekends, and spend morning and evening in prayer, you still won't be able to earn God's love.

God's love for you isn't based on performance. It's not rooted in how beautiful or popular, smart or successful you are. Instead, His love for you is like the love a father has for his children. It is a love that is yours simply because you are *you*.

Of course, God is delighted when you serve the church, the needy, and the sick. He wants you to be more and more like Him, and He is grieved when you sin. But regardless of your actions, His love does not waver and it does not change. You can rest in that promise, child of God.

Father, remind me that in trying to earn Your love, I am doubting Your grace—and forgive me!

Beating the Monday Blues

I'm ready, God, so ready, ready from head to toe, ready to sing,
ready to raise a tune: "Wake up, soul! Wake up, harp! wake up,
lute! Wake up, you sleepyhead sun!"

—Psalm 57:7–8 THE MESSAGE

Even though Monday is simply another day of the week, it can be a difficult day at times. It's the beginning of the week, and after a weekend away from the weekly routine, going back to the everyday may seem a little depressing. Lots of people struggle with the "Monday blues," but they can be overcome.

Often, those Monday morning blues are caused by the realization that the time of resting is over—but it doesn't have to be. Keep your heart focused on the Lord and not on the upcoming week.

"How?" you ask. Carve out time to simply sit with the Lord and pray. Reflect on His goodness. Lay your anxieties down before Him. Lean on His strength and not your own.

Yes, Monday is still there. And, yes, you still have to start the week. But rest can happen any day and at any time—if you're resting in the Lord. Ask Him to help you beat those Monday blues.

Help me rest this day, Lord, even in the midst of all its busyness.

Fear of Missing Out

I will tend them in a good pasture, and the mountain heights of Israel will be their grazing land. There they will lie down in good grazing land, and there they will feed in a rich pasture on the mountains of Israel.

—Ezekiel 34:14

We can sleep when we're dead." Perhaps you've seen that phrase on billboards, social media, or even on a T-shirt. It's a funny saying—at least on the surface—but taken seriously, that mind-set can lead you to exhaustion.

Approaching life in that way may seem adventurous and exciting. The world is your oyster, and there are so many things to see, taste, and experience. But, at the heart of it, that mind-set undervalues rest. It views rest as something negative. And it suggests that if you take time out to rest and rejuvenate, then you're missing out on life.

Don't believe it. Don't feel guilty if you can't do it all. You know your limits, and you know that in order to be a functioning, healthy person, you need rest. Don't succumb to the fear of missing out. Instead, rest in the Lord—and He'll bless you with an adventure-filled life.

I praise You, Lord, for leading me to rest and restoring my soul.

Rest in the Lord's Strength

I can do all things through him who strengthens me.

—Philippians 4:13 ESV

You rub your weary eyes and take another sip of coffee. You didn't know it was possible to feel this tired, and it's dragging you down. Are you feeling drained? Is life getting the best of you? Find rest in the Lord's strength.

Isaiah 40 says, "Even youths grow tired and weary, and young men stumble and fall; but those who hope in the LORD will renew their strength. They will soar on wings like eagles; they will run and not grow weary, they will walk and not be faint" (vv. 30–31). Everyone gets weary at some point—even the young. Life can be exhausting and hard, busy and overwhelming. But God has the power to renew your strength.

Collapse in the arms of your Maker and Provider. Let Him lift you up, lead you by quiet waters, and restore your soul. For just a moment, stop and simply sit with Him. Let Him strengthen your weary heart.

How sweet to collapse into Your arms, my Maker! Thank You for strengthening me when I'm weary.

Rest Isn't Selfish

Since we live by the Spirit, let us keep in step with the Spirit.

—Galatians 5:25

But I should be doing something. Does that thought ever creep in when you try to rest? Do you feel selfish for wanting time to yourself? Friend, it is not selfish; it's needed.

Maybe you're a busy parent, a graduate student, a business owner, or an active member of your church or community. There will always be things you "should" or "could" be doing, but rest is crucial to ensuring you're able to do everything else well.

Take a few minutes for yourself today. Perhaps it will be sneaking in a nap while the children are napping—even if it means you pick up takeout for dinner. Maybe it could be taking a break from studying to enjoy the fresh air. Or maybe you could say no to another project when you're feeling stretched too thin. Find a time of solitude, and strengthen yourself with rest today.

When You rested on earth, Jesus, did You think of me, knowing I would need Your example? Thank You for Your wisdom.

A Weekend for Rest

Let him sit alone in silence, for the LORD has laid it on him.

—Lamentations 3:28

What does your typical weekend look like? Weekends are a great time for connecting with friends, going out on the town, and enjoying more time with your children or family. But they also tend to be filled with cleaning, soccer games, grocery shopping, errands, and endless odd jobs. Basically, anything you weren't able to finish during the week spills over into the weekend.

Do you ever feel tired just thinking about your weekend? Perhaps it's time for you to incorporate a little more rest.

Even amid the hustle and bustle of running errands, cleaning the floors, and fixing that leaky pipe, you can carve out much-needed time to settle your mind and heart. Yes, there are things that need doing, but remember that slowing down is also one of them. Take time to rest before another week unfolds.

As I approach the weekend, God, show me how to rest more and to be busy less.

......

A Shift in Perspective

Your word is a lamp for my feet, a light on my path.

—Psalm 119:105

Have you ever been on a retreat? Do you remember the last time you worshipped God with full abandon? Have you ever noticed how different your mind-set became after you took a nap? Rest puts things into perspective.

When you do things such as go on an overnight retreat, lose yourself in worship, or allow your physical body to rest, you give your mind and heart a chance to recalibrate. Stepping away from busyness is so beneficial; it allows you to see the whole picture rather than get lost in a dizzying blur of activity.

Today, allow rest in God's Word to give you a new perspective. Soak up the Lord's words and let Scripture transform your mind. Listen—*really* listen—to the words of your favorite worship song. Take time for the rest you so desperately crave, and then watch as your perspective shifts and your thoughts begin to align more closely with those of Christ.

Thank You for the gift of rest, Father. It puts everything into perspective.

Are We There Yet?

For the vision is yet for the appointed [future] time. It hurries toward the goal [of fulfillment]; it will not fail. Even though it delays, wait [patiently] for it, because it will surely come; it will not delay.

—Habakkuk 2:3 AMP

Any parent knows that taking a trip with children means fielding this question at least a dozen times: "Are we there yet?" And the answer often sounds like this: "No, we're still in the driveway," or "We've been in the car for ten minutes—we have ten more hours." The ridiculousness of the question makes us laugh, but the truth is, we often ask the same question of God.

When we're in a waiting period, we want to know when we'll arrive at our destination. "Is this suffering almost over, Lord?" "How much longer will this take?" "I've been waiting forever." Like impatient children, we don't understand that it often takes time to reach the good places in life.

So the next time you're tempted to ask the Lord, "Are we there yet?" remind yourself instead of His perfect timing. And if the answer is "Not yet," settle back and rest, knowing that He is the Master Driver.

I trust that You're working out a perfect plan, Jesus. Give me the patience to endure the journey.

Fight the Rush

Be joyful in hope, patient in affliction, faithful in prayer.

—Romans 12:12

Rushing has become the norm in today's culture. We rush from meeting to meeting, incessantly checking our e-mail in between. We rush the kids to school, to doctor's appointments, and to after-school activities. We rush home to dinner and time with the family, or we rush to a dinner date with friends, out of breath and five minutes late.

What would your life look like without rushing? It's not easy to slow down, but it's possible. It must be done with intention and reliance on God, because living life at a slower pace doesn't come naturally. With practice, however, it can begin to feel natural.

How can you slow down today? Give yourself five more minutes to eat breakfast; taste the food instead of shoveling it down. Leave work early enough to beat rush-hour traffic and arrive home relaxed rather than tense. Choose one way to slow down today—and take a rest from the rush.

Instead of rushing and stress, please give me stillness and peace, Father God.

Find a Getaway

I will say of the LORD, "He is my refuge and my fortress, my God, in whom I trust."

—Psalm 91:2

In our busy, active, filled-to-the-brim lives, it may seem impossible to find a getaway—a place you can go that shelters you from the stressors, frustrations, and demands of today. But, weary traveler, consider this: the Lord can be your getaway.

He can shelter you from life's storms and protect you from danger. The Lord longs to relieve you of your burdens, and He invites you to set them down as soon as you enter His presence. He wants you to look to Him for strength. With His help, you'll find that the demands of today become less pressing and less intimidating.

Ask your Father to be your getaway, your place to hide from the busyness of the world. Run to Him and relax in His arms. Find joy in the fact that you can always, *always* retreat in Him. The Lord is your safe place. In Him, find refuge, comfort, and rest.

Shelter me from life's storms, Jesus. Be my getaway in this noisy, demanding life.

Count Your Blessings

Now, our God, we give you thanks, and praise your glorious name.
—1 Chronicles 29:13

How often do you stop to count your blessings? It is easy, so very easy, to look at all that we don't have. But a life of constant wanting leads to a life of constant striving. Be encouraged to find rest through thanksgiving today.

When you choose to focus on all that you *do* have, from the tiniest blessings to the biggest, your heart can't help but rejoice. A cool shower after an afternoon in the sun, a car that safely transports you to work, healthy children, food on the table—these are daily blessings.

Pause for a few minutes today and give thanks to the Lord, for He is good. All the good things in your life are His blessings to you—from the fragrant roses in your front yard to your closest confidant. He is a good God who loves to give good gifts to His children. Rest in thanksgiving today.

For all Your blessings, love, and mercy, I give thanks to You, Most High God.

Summer Rest

Winter is past, the rain has stopped; flowers cover the earth, it's time to sing. The cooing of doves is heard in our land. Fig trees are bearing fruit, while blossoms on grapevines fill the air with perfume.

—Song of Solomon 2:11–13 CEV

Summer is the time for sticky popsicles, the smell of fresh-cut grass, sandy toes, and burgers fresh off the grill. The days are longer, and the nights are warmer.

Summer is also a busy time, with vacations, pool dates, golf outings, and neighborhood block parties. Then, before you know it, summer is almost gone. But do you end the summer feeling rested?

This summer, make rest a priority. Enjoy a walk during a balmy summer evening. Sneak outside after the kids are in bed and simply gaze up at the stars. Settle everyone—even the kids—for a time of quiet reading each day. Say no to a golf outing in order to spend a morning in solitude.

The summer months show God's gorgeous creation in full, vivid bloom—let your eyes see, your ears hear, and your mouth taste the blessings and beauty of it all. Find rest in this summer season.

Thank You for summertime, Father. And help me rest in the beautiful warmth of Your creation.

Give Others Rest

From the ends of the earth I call to you, I call as my heart grows faint; lead me to the rock that is higher than I.

—Psalm 61:2

There is a time to find rest for yourself, and there's also a time to help others rest. You may be in a season where you feel rested, and you're able to make space in your life to lend a hand to others. If you're in that place, look around— there are always people who could use your help.

Do you know any new moms? Offer to bring them a meal. Is a colleague battling to keep up with work? Ask if he or she needs some assistance. Did your friend just have surgery? Offer to run errands or help around the house. Perhaps your pastor seems worn down; write a note of encouragement.

Rest is sorely needed in our culture today. From working moms to stay-at-home dads, students and teachers, friends and relatives, being busy and overloaded is a battle many are fighting. Can you help others find rest today?

Remind me that I can offer rest to those around me, dear Lord.

When Storms Roll In

Then He arose and rebuked the wind, and said to the sea, "Peace, be still!" And the wind ceased and there was a great calm.

—Mark 4:39 NKJV

The forecast for your life looks bleak. You can see that there is pain, stress, suffering, or turmoil ahead. Your shoulders begin to hunch against the burden, and your heart races in fear. You're just not sure if you're strong enough for a storm this big.

When you see storm clouds rolling into your life, you may feel completely beaten. You might feel angry or sad, confused or afraid. And you may even wonder how in the world you'll get through it all. Here is your answer: take refuge in the Lord.

Your Father in heaven might not stop the storm from coming. But He will walk through it with you. So even if the circumstances around you look treacherous, you can tell your heart, *Peace, be still*, because Jesus is with you in the boat of life. Settle into His protective arms, and rest knowing that He provides respite and refuge.

You are my Rock, my Redeemer, and my Refuge, Jesus. Thank You for Your strength in my life.

Weary of Complaining?

Shout for joy to the LORD, all the earth. Worship the LORD with gladness; come before him with joyful songs. Know that the LORD is God. It is he who made us, and we are his; we are his people, the sheep of his pasture.

—Psalm 100:1–3

A complaining heart gets wearisome over time. Have you ever noticed how you feel when you're constantly complaining? You become defensive and critical; you feel bitter and frustrated. Instead of enjoying the day, you are constantly finding one more thing to moan and groan about—and though it may feel therapeutic for a moment, it only serves to drag you down.

Dear friend, a complaining heart is a weary heart. Peace is far from you, and contentment is nowhere to be found. It's a difficult way to live.

Lay down your arsenal of complaints. Surrender your weapons of anger and criticism. Take a small step toward gratitude; ask the Father to help you rest in contentment instead of wallowing in complaining. He wants to satisfy your soul and refresh you with His presence. Let Him change your heart and turn your complaining to rejoicing.

I surrender my complaining heart to You, Father. Replace it with a heart of praise for You.

Accept the Invitation

*God is awesome in his sanctuary. The God of Israel gives power
and strength to his people. Praise be to God!*

—Psalm 68:35 NLT

What are your priorities? God, family, church, children, work, school, and friends are all common priorities. We prioritize what we feel is important, and the rest falls by the wayside and is picked up when—or if—we have time. Too often, we forget to prioritize rest. Perhaps because it doesn't feel like a tangible and pressing part of our life, we put it on the back burner.

Rest doesn't often happen by accident. It doesn't seek us out or demand our attention. Instead, rest waits as an invitation—and we need to actively accept the invitation.

What would it look like to accept that invitation today? What can you say no to that will allow you say yes to rest? If it just doesn't seem possible, remember this invitation that Christ extended to His disciples: "Come with me by yourselves to a quiet place and get some rest" (Mark 6:31).

*When I am invited to rest, Lord, help me gladly accept the
invitation.*

The Best Version of Yourself

For the foolishness of God is wiser than human wisdom, and the weakness of God is stronger than human strength.

—1 Corinthians 1:25

want to be a better parent." "I want to have a better job." "I want to get better grades." "I want to be a more loving son."

There are so many ways we can better ourselves, and as Christians, we should try to be the best we can be. We need to do our best to be a good mother or father, neighbor or friend, sister or brother, colleague or boss. And yes, we need to do all things as if we're doing them for God. But we also should acknowledge this truth: we can't be the best at everything.

Do you ever feel overwhelmed by everything you want—or feel you need—to excel at? Bring these concerns to the Lord. He knows exactly what you need, and He is able to help you see what is truly important. And He can gently, patiently, and tenderly transform you into the best version of yourself. Find rest by trusting in Him.

I want to be transformed, Lord, but I need Your help to do it.

Fill Your Cup

May the Lord direct your hearts into God's love and Christ's perseverance.

—2 Thessalonians 3:5

Imagine you have an early morning breakfast meeting. You wake to your alarm, get dressed, and head out with visions of strong black coffee. When you sit down at the table, a cup of steaming coffee is placed in front of you. You take a sip. It's good.

The meeting begins, and your cup is half full. The waiter asks if you'd like a refill, but then adds only hot water to your cup. In fact, each time he refills your cup, he adds only water, not coffee. Soon, the coffee is only a memory floating in a cup of light brown water. And you're left feeling frustrated and cheated.

The same thing can happen with rest. You may begin your week strong and ready to take on the world. But if you make only halfhearted attempts to rest, you're going to feel watered down by the end of the week. Make it a point to refill with true rest this week.

Lord, remind me to refill with true rest—and with You—instead of watered-down substitutes.

Without Shame or Guilt

Let your face shine on your servant; save me in your unfailing love.
—Psalm 31:16

Because rest is important for our spiritual growth, Satan will do everything he can to keep us busy and distracted. One of the most common ways he ensures we don't rest is through guilt. Do you ever feel guilty if you take time to rest?

God worked for six days. He formed tall, sturdy oaks, poured light into fireflies, and made man in His own image—and then, He rested. Without guilt and without shame. The Lord worked, and then He rested. The Lord did it as an example for His children.

When we rest, we aren't neglecting our duties, and we aren't being lazy. But we are giving our souls a chance to breathe and redirecting our minds to thoughts of the Lord. Rest benefits our physical bodies and our spiritual being. It should be met with thanksgiving, not guilt. Give thanks that the Lord knew we needed rest, and so He created it at the beginning of time.

Take away my shame and guilt, dear Jesus, and help me enjoy the blessing of rest.

Restore and Renew

For the sake of my family and friends, I will say, "Peace be within you."

When Jesus drew away from the crowds and found a place alone to pray, He was resting with His Father. He did it on purpose and with intention. How often do you find yourself resting intentionally and on purpose? And no, falling asleep on the couch doesn't count! Only intentional rest brings true restoration.

You have permission to intentionally rest today, friend. Sit with a cup of coffee for a few extra minutes. Take some time for an afternoon stroll through the park. Put aside your responsibilities this evening, and enjoy some quality time with your spouse instead.

Continual work will leave you worn out and empty, but purposefully seeking out rest will bless you with restoration and renewal for your soul.

Restore my soul and renew my body. Father, please draw near to me.

Rest in Being Uniquely You

So God created mankind in his own image, in the image of God he created them; male and female he created them.

—Genesis 1:27

Ponder this question: What is your favorite thing about yourself? Is it your unique laugh or the color of your eyes? Is it your contagious love for others or your mathematical mind? Maybe you love your ability to run or your quiet confidence. There are many things to love about yourself—after all, you were created in the image of a perfect God!

There are also things that make you unique—things that you may not be quite so fond of. Do you have funny-shaped feet or a tendency to turn bright red when embarrassed? Do you carry the family nose or cry at the drop of a hat? Your uniqueness isn't bad, and it's not something to fix.

Stop trying to hide or change those unique things about you—they make up *you*, and *you* are beloved by God. Rest in accepting who you are today.

Father, help me rest in my uniqueness and take pleasure in the quirks that make me, me!

JULY

Restore to me the joy of your salvation
and grant me a willing spirit, to sustain me.

—Psalm 51:12

A Time to Rest

"For six years you are to sow your fields and harvest the crops, but during the seventh year let the land lie unplowed and unused."

—Exodus 23:10–11

In the summer, the fields are bursting with rows of golden corn, and prickly blackberry bushes are heavy with sweet fruit. Zucchini and cucumbers grow large, sugar snap peas beg to be eaten, and peaches hang low. The fruit of the land is plentiful in summertime.

But every land needs a time to rest, and in resting, it will grow more fruitful. Yes, it will be used again, but first, the land needs to lie still.

Isn't that exactly the way we operate? If we are continually producing, pouring ourselves out, serving, and working, we become less fruitful. We juggle too many balls until—one by one—they all begin to drop. We become a dry and weary land. Rest is important, friends, and finding time to rest is certainly not a sign of weakness; it's a sign of true wisdom. Is it time for you to lie fallow and rest for a while?

Is it time for me to lie fallow, Lord? Show me how You would like me to rest.

Perfect Timing

Oh, the depth of the riches of the wisdom and knowledge of God!
How unsearchable his judgments, and his paths beyond tracing out!
—Romans 11:33

Dear friend, are you learning the hard truth that God's timing is not like your own? Are you anxious to see your prayers answered? Or frustrated that nothing is happening the way you thought it would? Rest assured, you are not alone. We have all struggled with understanding God's timing at one point or another, but here's the reassuring truth: God is in control, He loves you as His own child, and He'll always do what is ultimately best for you.

Just as a father loves to give good gifts to his children, the Lord loves to bless you. You can rest in His plans because He is your loving and generous Father, because He'll be with you every step of the way, and because His plans are better than any plan you could devise for yourself. Let go of the reins, and rest instead in God's promises, plans, and perfect timing.

Father, I believe Your plans are better than my own. Help me see that truth.

Allow Rest

Cast all your anxiety on him because he cares for you.

—1 Peter 5:7

You need to rest, but you keep pressing forward, hoping that somehow, someday you'll catch up on your sleep. But how long have you been telling yourself you'll rest, only to find that—months later—you're still trying to catch up? To finally get the rest you're craving, you must first *allow* yourself to rest.

Rest looks different for everyone. For some, it's taking a sabbatical or extended vacation. For others, it's a nap or an hour of solitude. You know your needs and your limits— what would good, adequate rest look like for you? Make a plan, write it down, and commit to it—perhaps even ask a friend or your spouse to hold you accountable.

You need rest—we all do. It's not a sign of weakness; it's simply part of being human. Give yourself a break. Decide when and how you will rest and then allow yourself to do it.

I'm not good at allowing myself to rest, Lord. Show me a plan that will work for me.

Freedom in Jesus

Cast your cares on the Lord and he will sustain you; he will never let the righteous be shaken.

—Psalm 55:22

What is weighing heavily on your heart today, friend? Do you feel especially anxious about anything? Do you feel discouraged or frustrated about a particular situation? The Lord desires to give you rest from those burdens. He wants to free you from any anxiety or worry, and He wants to bless you with His peace, joy, and hope.

Whatever your worry—about yourself or a loved one, about health or money, about spiritual concerns—the Lord knows and cares. He lovingly tells us to bring Him those burdens and worries, and He will take them on. Instead of feeling buried under the weight of anxiety, you can experience the freedom of hope.

Turn to Jesus. He knows you are worried and tired, and He longs for you to come to Him . . . so that He can give you rest.

Lord Jesus, I bring my worries to You, and I trust You to take control.

God's Big Promises

"So do not fear, for I am with you; do not be dismayed, for I am your God. I will strengthen you and help you; I will uphold you with my righteous right hand."

—Isaiah 41:10

God gives us big promises in the Bible: He promises never to leave or forsake us. He promises redemption and restoration to those who follow Him. And He promises that He has great plans and big dreams for us—greater than we could ever imagine. He declares that we are His masterpieces.

All of the Lord's promises are so good and so true, yet we live as though He's lying. We live frantically—striving and struggling to achieve our goals, prove ourselves, and attain approval. We say yes to too many things and no to too few for fear that others won't like us. Simply put, we aren't resting in God's promises.

The Lord tells us not to worry or be anxious; He'll provide for our every need. He tells us He delights in us, for we are His sons and daughters. How miraculous! How wonderful! Rest in the enduring, eternal, and perfect promises of God today.

Teach me to rest; teach me to trust; teach me to delight in Your love for me, Father.

The Sun Will Rise

May our Lord Jesus Christ himself and God our Father . . .
encourage your hearts and strengthen you in every good deed
and word.

—2 Thessalonians 2:16–17

When the sun sets and you fall into bed after a particularly rough day, do you ever feel as if the whole world is against you? Your kids are demanding, your work is stressing you out, your responsibilities are overwhelming, and everything would be so much better if you just had a little more time. Sound familiar?

Rest assured, after every bad night there is a new sunrise, every frustrating day can be followed by a joyful evening, and each bad start can end with a fantastic finish. When God says His mercies are new every morning, He means it. He has more than enough grace for you each day. You can be sure of it—as sure as the sun rises. Find peace today knowing that God gives you new beginnings . . . over and over and over again.

Thank You, Jesus, for Your grace upon grace—every morning,
evening, and moment in between.

Feed Your Body with Rest

And my God will meet all your needs according to the riches of his glory in Christ Jesus.

—Philippians 4:19

When you look over the course of your day, are there times for rest? Are there moments you can catch your breath, sit down, and reflect? Or are you going, going, and going until you drop into bed an hour later than you'd hoped?

Dear friend, you need to rest *every day*. It might seem productive to rush around nonstop, but your body, mind, and soul were not created to function that way. Daily rest is needed, just like daily bread. If you skip eating, your body ends up depleted. In the same way, skipping rest leaves your body weak and deeply weary.

Take time each day to rest, incorporating it into your daily routine. Follow the example of Jesus, who made an effort to rest even when thousands of people were looking to Him to be fed. Yes, He fed them with loaves and fishes, but then He also fed Himself with solitude, prayer, and rest (Matthew 14:23).

Jesus, help me follow Your example of taking time to rest.

Joy from the Lord

He has shown you, O mortal, what is good. And what does the
LORD require of you? To act justly and to love mercy and to walk
humbly with your God.

—Micah 6:8

We are bombarded with advertisements at every turn. Our mailboxes are stuffed with flyers, television shows are interrupted with commercials, streaming music services blare ads every few songs, and magazines show us all the things we don't have.

It's easy to see why we're never satisfied with what we have. We are constantly assaulted by voices that tell us we won't be happy unless we have (fill in the blank). And, if we're not careful, we'll begin to believe these messages. But, truthfully, we'll never find contentment in new clothes or the latest gadget. True contentment, and true rest, are found only in Christ.

Today, be mindful of the messages you believe. Every time you think, *I would be happy if I just had . . .* , ask the Lord to reveal His truth to you. You'll find rest for your soul not by accumulating possessions, but by immersing yourself in the Lord.

Dear Lord, remind me that my joy comes not from things, but from
You and You alone.

Glorious Summer

Ask the animals, and they will teach you, or the birds in the sky, and they will tell you; or speak to the earth, and it will teach you, or let the fish in the sea inform you. Which of all these does not know that the hand of the LORD has done this? In his hand is the life of every creature and the breath of all mankind.

—Job 12:7–10

God's creation is glorious in summer. Flowers are in full bloom, and the air is rich with their perfume. Plump tomatoes appear in the garden, and vibrant butterflies float along on the breeze. Ocean waves refresh and renew, the sand is warm, and the evenings are perfect for stargazing. There's nothing quite like summer.

The Lord's handiwork is there for you to enjoy. Its beauty directs your thoughts to the creative hand of God, and its splendor is unmatched. Even if you're busy, even if your schedule is demanding and your free time scarce, take a moment to be mindful of God's creation. Let nature refresh your spirit and calm your anxious heart. Take time, dear friend, to walk by the still, quiet waters and to feel the love of your great Shepherd. Rest in God's creation.

Lord, thank You for creating such a gorgeous world—to You be all the glory.

Shutting Out Impatience

A person's wisdom yields patience; it is to one's glory to overlook an offense.

—Proverbs 19:11

H*urry up. What's taking you so long? I'm waiting on you again.* Have you often found yourself saying these things? Perhaps you directed them at a colleague or a spouse or a child. Maybe you were exasperated with your mom or your brother. Or perhaps you even shouted these things at God when He was slow to reveal an answer.

While some people are naturally patient, most of us have to work at it again and again. But over time and through prayer, you can calm your impatient heart and find a deep well of patience. Cultivating patience will allow you to wait instead of act, ask instead of demand, and trust the Lord's plan instead of forging ahead with your own. Patience means that when things don't happen exactly according to your schedule, you're able to handle it gracefully. Choosing patience instead of impatience will reward you with rest and peace. No, it won't always be easy, but it will always be worth it.

Father, please change my impatience to patience, my skepticism to trust, and my frustration to peace.

Linger and Enjoy

Who compares with you among gods, O GOD? Who compares with you in power, in holy majesty, in awesome praises, wonder-working God?

—Exodus 15: 11 THE MESSAGE

Children are the best at enjoying the small things—a solitary bubble, a caterpillar, a balloon, a ride on the lawn mower, a dandelion. It doesn't matter if it's a tiny puddle or a huge swimming pool, a trip to the shoe store or to Disney World, kids are able to see even the smallest of moments and things as opportunities for wonder and joy.

When did we lose that? When did we become so hard to impress and so difficult to captivate? Every day we rush past so many tiny but great moments simply because we're too busy or too distracted.

Give yourself permission to slow down today. Let your gaze linger over the sunrise, savor that delicious lunch with all your senses, and be on the lookout for the amazing and beautiful. God has placed it all around you. Open your eyes, and rest in its wonder.

Lord, help me slow down, refocus, and be on the lookout for Your wonders all the around me.

Ask for Help

[Do not] give up meeting together, as some are in the habit of doing, but encouraging one another—and all the more as you see the Day approaching.

—Hebrews 10:25

It's not easy to ask for help. Our culture prides itself on self-sufficiency. We look with envy at the those who seem to "do it all." Asking for help may make us feel weak or embarrassed, and we don't want to burden others with our needs.

Asking for help requires vulnerability. But by taking a risk and being vulnerable, you encourage others to be vulnerable too. And wouldn't you like to have people around you who are open about their struggles rather than just putting on a brave face every day? It might be up to you to begin the movement.

Ask someone in your circle for help. It might be a best friend, a coworker, or a spouse. It may be someone from church or from your small group, an aunt, a cousin, or a sibling. You don't need to be ashamed. In fact, you'll probably find you aren't alone in your struggles. So ask for help, and when help arrives, rest.

It's hard to ask for help, Lord. Please give me the courage to be vulnerable.

God, the Giver of Rest

The Lord is my helper; I will not be afraid. What can mere mortals do to me?

—Hebrews 13:6

When you hold tightly to your own plans, hopes, and dreams, you exhaust yourself. Why? Because you're pursuing your path according to your own strength, and your own strength is finite. It is limited. You are only human—you are not invincible—and your resources, though they may seem vast at times, are so very small when compared to the Lord's.

Trust in the Lord. His plans are bigger, better, and more beautiful than you could ever imagine. He doesn't want you to walk around worried and burdened and overwhelmed; instead, He wants you to rest in Him. Let God call the shots, make the plan, and work all things out to your good. Follow Him in complete trust. God alone is the Giver of gifts and the Giver of rest.

Lord, doing things my own way is exhausting. Teach me to trust You and Your plans.

In the Dark of Night

You'll have no more need of the sun by day nor the brightness of the moon at night. GOD *will be your eternal light.*

—Isaiah 60:19 THE MESSAGE

Have you ever found yourself in pitch-black darkness, unable to see where you're going? You strain your eyes, feel around with your hands, and tense your muscles while trying not to trip or stumble. You can't relax because you're not sure where you are.

But what if someone were guiding you by the hand *and* you had a flashlight? Your experience would be totally different, wouldn't it? You'd be able to see the way ahead. It would be much less stressful.

Dear friend, the Lord is guiding you. His Word is a lamp for your feet, a light for your way. He knows exactly how to get you where you need to go, and He is the most trustworthy guide; He has an aerial view. You can have peace, knowing that the Creator of the universe is guiding you along in His perfect, redemptive plan. You can find rest, even in the darkness.

Lord, teach me to trust Your leading instead of fumbling around on my own.

God's Word Speaks

*The Spirit of the Lord shall rest upon him, the Spirit of wisdom,
understanding, counsel, and might; the Spirit of knowledge and of
the fear of the Lord.*

—Isaiah 11:2 TLB

There are many examples of rest in Scripture, beginning
with the creation of the world, which included a day of
rest for the Lord. Later, in the Ten Commandments, God
commanded His people to rest. And when Jesus came, He
taught His disciples to rest and even rested Himself in the
midst of His busy ministry.

When we say that Scripture is a guide for our life, that
means we abide by its teachings—and one very important part of those teachings is to rest. God doesn't mean
everyone else should rest, but not you. No, He speaks of
rest for your sake too. He wants you to stop rushing, stressing, and tiring yourself out.

Ask the Lord to show you how to rest. Search the Bible
for verses about rest, and follow their teachings. Then you
will certainly find rest for your soul.

*Father, will You show me specific Bible verses I can live by in order
to pursue a more restful life?*

A Pause on Pleasing

The Lord looks down from heaven on all mankind to see if there are any who are wise, who want to please God.

—Psalm 14:2 TLB

'm disappointed in you. I was counting on you. I needed you, and you weren't there. Those are hard words to hear. Some people so dread disappointing others that they strive to please everyone all the time. They work and work and then work some more to make sure everyone is happy.

But trying to please everyone is exhausting—and impossible. Admit it: you *can't* make everyone happy. Of course, you can say yes to some things, but it's not your duty to say yes to all things. Sometimes you simply need to say no to others and yes to God and yourself. Putting God first and giving some priority to nourishing your own body and soul are actually key components in being able to serve others well.

Do you need to put a pause on pleasing others today? Ask the Lord to help you put pleasing Him at the top of your to-do list.

Jesus, help me establish healthy boundaries and remind me to focus on You first and foremost.

Living in Light of Eternity

"God did not send his Son into the world to condemn the world,
but to save the world through him."

—John 3:17

When your perspective shifts to an eternal viewpoint, suddenly a lot of once-important things fall to the wayside. In light of eternity, many of our daily stressors or worries simply become insignificant.

Of course, it's all too easy to get caught up in your children's extracurricular activities. It's common to be ultra-focused on your resume, making sure it's one that will dazzle any prospective employer. Your job helps pay the bills, and you want to ensure job security, so you work all hours of the day and night. Life is busy, and there are lots of important matters pulling you in every direction. Many of them are good. But, in light of eternity, they aren't necessarily life-and-death concerns.

If you find yourself consumed by busyness, frazzled and frantic in getting everything done, look to the Lord. Ask Him to clear your vision and your mind. And try to look at your day with an eternal perspective.

God, remind me that this life is simply a blip in time, and eternity is what truly matters.

Being a Restful Friend

A friend loves at all times, and is born, as is a brother, for adversity.

—Proverbs 17:17 AMPC

When your friends think of you, what words might pop into their minds? Hopefully, they'd think of words like *loyal*, *loving*, *encouraging*, *sacrificial*, and *compassionate*. But have you considered that your friends may describe you as *too busy*, *stressed*, or even *stressful*?

Ultimately, we should strive to be friends who offer encouragement and who help others find rest for themselves. For those we love, we should be a peaceful port of refuge when the storms of life hit; we should be givers and not merely takers.

If you are realizing that you may not be a restful friend, be encouraged. Jesus can help you be that type of friend. Call on Him and ask Him to show you how to love your friends well, how to model a life of rest, and how to have a heart that reflects true rest in the Lord.

Jesus, teach me to be a restful friend—a safe place for others to rest.

Easing Expectations

Therefore, since we are surrounded by such a great cloud of witnesses, let us throw off everything that hinders and the sin that so easily entangles. And let us run with perseverance the race marked out for us.

—Hebrews 12:1

You wanted to finish that big project at work, vacuum your home, take the car to the shop, check in with your dad, cook dinner, and get ahead on your Bible study. But none of those things happened, and you're left feeling really discouraged. We've all had those sorts of days.

Sometimes you may need to adjust your expectations. They may simply be too high, and you run the risk of getting stuck in a vicious cycle of unmet expectations and disappointment. It's okay, at times, to throw your hands up and say, "I'll try again tomorrow."

Is it time to ease up on your expectations a little? Would it really be disastrous if you didn't finish everything today? God promises to always take care of you—and that promise doesn't end if your to-do list isn't finished. Let go of your expectations today, and instead, ask God to help you look at your day through the lens of *His* expectations.

God, help me adjust my expectations and live according to Your plans, not my own.

World Weary

Now to him who is able to do far more abundantly than all that we
ask or think, according to the power at work within us, to him be
glory in the church and in Christ Jesus throughout all generations,
forever and ever. Amen.

—Ephesians 3:20–21 ESV

Are you feeling a little world weary, dear traveler? Does it seem as if everything around you is falling apart, and you're left standing in the rubble feeling very alone and more than a little broken and bruised? Take heart—the Lord is with you.

Even in the midst of the chaos, brokenness, and trials of today, God is standing with you. And not only is He standing with you, He's clearing a path for you—a path that is God-ordained and holy. You can let go of fear and worry, for the Lord is at work, and all you need to do is cling to Him. There's no need to be anxious, nor do you need to despair. The Lord—incredibly mighty and Ruler of all—is close to the brokenhearted, the weary, and the troubled. You only need be still. Breathe in His presence, for He is with you.

Oh, Father, sometimes this world's brokenness is too much for me.
I'm so grateful You are near.

It's Time

Do you not know that your bodies are temples of the Holy Spirit, who is in you, whom you have received from God? You are not your own.

—1 Corinthians 6:19

You may feel that self-care is a little indulgent or even selfish. Why take a nap when you could be mowing the lawn? Why sit in the stillness of the morning when you should be packing lunches? But the truth is, more often than not, self-care results in a healthier, more productive and giving you. Because you're taking time to be fed, you're better able to face the day with strength rather than weariness.

How can you give yourself some self-care today? Eat lunch at the park instead of your desk. Take a half-day to do some gardening or fishing or whatever rejuvenates your soul. Spend time in quiet meditation on God's Word. There are so many ways to care for yourself, and if you need rest, it's not selfish to ask for it or act on it. Challenge yourself to rest in a little self-care this week. It really is important.

It's easy for me to neglect myself, Father. Will You help me make space for self-care this week?

Seasons Change

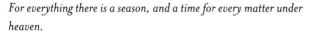

For everything there is a season, and a time for every matter under heaven.

—Ecclesiastes 3:1 ESV

What season of life are you experiencing right now? Are you enjoying a summer of joy and delight? Do you feel rich with blessings? Or maybe you're in a season of winter when the icy winds chafe, storms buffet and bruise, and your soul is exposed and vulnerable, like the bare limbs of a tree. Or are you at last entering a season of spring after that long, hard winter? The air may feel chilly, but tender sprouts of hope are unfolding from the ground, reminding you that there is life after spiritual winter.

If you are in a difficult season, have courage. Seasons change. The sun will shine again; the Lord's goodness will chase the dark clouds away. You may not be able to change the weather or your circumstances, but you can protect yourself from the elements with prayer and Scripture and by surrounding yourself with people who love you. Take comfort in the promise that the rich blessings of summer are coming.

Lord, may I embrace the lessons and blessings of this season—and may I stand firm in Your love.

Laying Down Your Life

"Greater love has no one than this: to lay down one's life for one's friends."

—John 15:13

Do you feel as if you spend enough time with Jesus? Or are you always wishing you had more time in the day to truly be in His presence?

How often do you have some type of screen in front of your face, such as a television, phone, laptop, or tablet? Many of us would admit to having some sort of electronic device within our reach at all times. But, at times, it gets to be too much. It can easily take away our time of experiencing the Lord.

Have you laid down your technology for the Lord? John 15:13 talks about laying down one's life for friends—so, on a much smaller scale, would you be willing to lay down your electronic distractions for the greatest Friend of all, for even half an hour a day? That time with the Lord will be time well spent. You'll leave it feeling refreshed, full, and eager to tackle the day with the Lord Jesus at your side.

I want to lay down my distractions, Lord, and spend more time with You.

He Cares for You

Jesus replied: "'Love the Lord your God with all your heart and with all your soul and with all your mind.'"

—Matthew 22:37

Child of God, you have a perfect Friend, Comforter, and Redeemer. Jesus is your Refuge and Rock, Savior and Provider. He desires good things for you, and He loves you so much that He gave His life for you. He endured torture and cruelty because of His desire to bring you salvation. And even now He promises to carry your burdens, worries, and fears—simply because He cares for you.

Rest in the love of Christ today. Rest in His grace and mercy. Take comfort in the knowledge that He has defeated the enemy and sits at the right hand of God the Father. He longs to bring you rest, to rescue you from your weariness, and to call you friend.

Take joyful rest today in knowing that the love of Christ is deep and abiding, and it is for you.

Jesus, thank You for Your rich, abiding, and redemptive love.

Welcome, Silence

Tremble and do not sin; when you are on your beds, search your hearts and be silent.

—Psalm 4:4

In today's world, it's so easy to busy ourselves with distractions. We can turn to our phones, click the remote, put in some headphones, or turn on the computer. There is so much we can—and often do—turn to in order to fill the silence. But silence can be your place of rest.

Certainly, it can be almost frightening to let your world become still. It may seem easier to quiet your worries or insecurities with a funny sitcom or a Facebook binge. But what would happen if you simply sat? If you welcomed silence?

Thankfully, our God doesn't choose to distract Himself from our troubles; He faces them head-on and promises to come to your defense—"The LORD will fight for you; you need only to be still" (Exodus 14:14). Sit in silence and stillness with the Lord today. Don't mute your fears with the noise of distraction; let Him fight for you.

Lord Jesus, You are my strength and help in times of need. With You, I can face my fears.

An Act of Kindness

*By the seventh day God had finished his work. On the seventh day
he rested from all his work. God blessed the seventh day. He made
it a Holy Day because on that day he rested from his work, all the
creating God had done.*

—Genesis 2:2–3 THE MESSAGE

If you had one day to yourself, without any obligations,
what would you do? Read a book, take a nap, go out for
breakfast, or head to the park? Or maybe you'd immerse
yourself in a house project or take your grandkids to a
movie. Or perhaps you'd just want to watch television and
eat brownies—a rare luxury in your busy life.

Now, imagine doing these things even when you still
have all of life's usual obligations. Would you feel guilty?
Would you try to hide it? Friend, you'll always have some
sort of responsibility in life, but you still need to feed your
mind, body, and soul.

Give yourself permission to do something restful. It's a
needed act of kindness for yourself. Make rest a priority—in
whatever form you need it—and reflect on the goodness of
a God who loves His children enough to command them
to rest.

*God, sometimes rest feels frivolous and self-centered. Remind me
that it's okay to rest.*

Turn the Other Cheek

Bear with each other and forgive one another if any of you has a grievance against someone. Forgive as the Lord forgave you.

—Colossians 3:13

When others mistreat you, complaining may feel good at first, but often it will leave you feeling even more frustrated than before. Instead of complaining, consider giving grace.

If someone offends you, do you have the grace to turn the other cheek? When a friend annoys you or an acquaintance ticks you off, do you seek a solution—or someone to rant to? Yes, there are times when you need to confront, speak truth into others' lives, or gently educate them on their wrongdoings. But other times, *often times*, you simply need to give grace.

The next time you feel your temper rise or your frustration level increase, ask yourself if this is really an opportunity for grace. Maybe you just need to walk away, take a deep breath, and pray for guidance. Our Lord gives us grace upon grace; when you offer it to others, you will find a restful peace that passes understanding.

Lord, when I get frustrated with others, help me respond with forgiveness and grace.

Finding Assurance

Then Hannah prayed and said: "My heart rejoices in the LORD; in the LORD my horn is lifted high. My mouth boasts over my enemies, for I delight in your deliverance."

—1 Samuel 2:1

You've prayed for years. Your son isn't a believer; the marriage you long for hasn't come; you need a job; you can't beat this cancer. We all have prayers that seemingly go unanswered, and sometimes we wonder, *Is the Lord even listening?*

Yes, the Lord is listening. But His timing and plan are not always the same as your own. It's a difficult truth to accept, especially when you're praying for something good, something with eternal consequences. How, then, do you rest in the Lord?

There are no easy answers, but remember this truth: the same Jesus who gave His life for you, the same God who sent His Son to die for you, the same Holy Spirit who intercedes for you—hears your prayers. If God's love is so vast, deep, and wide, surely His plans for you are also good. Find rest in that love and in all that it promises.

It's so hard when prayers seem to go unanswered, Father. Help me trust in Your love and Your plan.

Off to a Good Start

Morning by morning he dispenses his justice, and every new day he does not fail.

—Zephaniah 3:5

Your morning often foreshadows what the rest of your day will look like. If you have a chaotic morning—rushing around, trying to get out of the door, spilling coffee on the way out—that tone can easily be carried throughout the rest of the day, making it difficult to find rest.

But consider this type of morning instead: you wake up before anyone else and sit with a cup of coffee or tea. You reflect on the Lord's goodness in your week, and you listen as He speaks to your heart. And your day begins in a restful, peaceful manner.

That kind of slow, still, peaceful morning is possible, but it requires a bit of sacrifice. It may mean extra planning the night before, an earlier bedtime, and an extra early ring from the alarm clock. But starting the day by putting your expectations, worries, and plans in the Lord's hands is the most restful way to begin.

I'm thankful I can come to You in the mornings, Father God. Fill my day with peace and rest.

The Gift of Rest

"My yoke is easy and my burden is light."

—Matthew 11:30

Watching the sun sink deep into the horizon. Walking in the stillness of the late afternoon. Taking a nap when you feel weary. Sitting with the Lord, the early birds, and a cup of coffee. All these things sound rather wonderful, don't they?

They are all acts of rest, and they are all available to you. The Lord wants you to take advantage of this rest. He wants you to incorporate it into your life, just as He took a day of rest after the creation of Adam and Eve. It wasn't that the Creator of the heavens and earth needed rest; rather, He was giving you an example of how to live.

Find joy in that example; take delight in the Lord who knows that we are fragile and human. He desires for you to stop your rushing and start your resting. He gives you good and wonderful gifts, and one of those gifts is rest.

Thank You for telling me it's okay to rest, Lord. What a wonderful gift!

No More Fast Food

When the hour came, Jesus and his apostles reclined at the table.

—Luke 22:14

When the Bible mentions Jesus eating, He is usually seen reclining. Even when eating with His enemies, the Pharisees, the Bible tells us He reclined (Luke 7:36). And when it was time for the Last Supper, Jesus gathered His closest friends, the disciples, into a room, and they reclined for the meal. Meals were not rushed or scrambling or eaten while working. Instead, mealtimes were opportunities for fellowship and restful rejuvenation.

What do meals look like in your life? Do you grab breakfast as you head out the door or eat lunch hunched over a computer? Is dinner eaten in front of the television or in the car? Life is busy, and it's often more convenient to eat *and* get something done. But, at least once a week, let your meal fill both your body and your soul. Linger at the table. Simply sit and eat. Break bread as you take a break from the rush and hurry.

Jesus, help me follow Your example, and let mealtime nourish both my body and soul.

AUGUST

Since we have been justified through faith,
we have peace with God through our Lord
Jesus Christ.

—Romans 5:1

It's Okay to Rest

The women who had been companions of Jesus from Galilee followed along. They saw the tomb where Jesus' body was placed. Then they went back to prepare burial spices and perfumes. They rested quietly on the Sabbath, as commanded.

—Luke 23:55–56 THE MESSAGE

As much as we'd like rest to be an integral part of our lives, it's often cast aside. Rest must be deliberately sought out, but we aren't always diligent about doing that. After all, our lives are busy and we simply don't have time to rest . . . or do we?

If your car broke down, you'd make time to take it to the mechanic. If your oven stopped working, you'd call someone to fix it. If you were hungry, you'd find time to eat. If you had a work deadline, you would work diligently to meet it. But if you're tired . . . do you rest?

Just like bringing the car to the mechanic or making time to eat, you need to make time to rest. Rest must be intentional, and it must be a priority. And once you do rest, you'll realize how much you needed it. It really is okay to carve out time to rest. Do it today.

It's hard to make time to rest, Lord. Please take away any guilt associated with resting today.

A Day Well Spent

"For my thoughts are not your thoughts, neither are your ways my ways," declares the LORD.

—Isaiah 55:8

We all love the feeling of ending a day filled with productivity. It feels good to know we've used our time well, crossed items off our to-do list, and accomplished a lot. Productivity is not bad; it's usually a sign of a good work ethic and an organized life. But if productivity becomes your idol, if checking items off your to-do list becomes your life goal, it's time to take a step back.

Life isn't simply about producing; it's also about living for the Lord, loving Him, and showing His love to others. Yes, God loves to see you use your talents and gifts, and He calls you to be a good steward of your resources and time. But He also desires your time and attention. And if you choose to put the Lord first in your day, it will have been a day well spent—regardless of what else gets done.

Father, help me focus on my relationship with You more than my accomplishments this day.

There Is Trouble, But . . .

Why, my soul, are you downcast? Why so disturbed within me? Put your hope in God, for I will yet praise him, my Savior and my God.

—Psalm 42:5

In John 16:33, Jesus told His followers, "I have told you these things, so that in me you may have peace. In this world you will have trouble. But take heart! I have overcome the world." If you're in a time of trouble, do not be dismayed and do not be discouraged; Jesus is not surprised by it.

If your heart is downcast and your burden feels heavy, Jesus wants you to do something radical: He wants you to give your burden to Him. He wants to take it from you so that you are no longer beaten down or afraid. What a gift! What a Savior!

Jesus wants you to have rest during the joyful times of your life, and He also wants to give you peace when you're walking through the storms. In Christ alone your hope is found—fall into His waiting arms. He can—and will—give rest to your soul.

Oh, Father, sometimes the storms overwhelm me. Thank You for the refuge of Your strong arms.

God Never Disappoints

We know that in all things God works for the good of those who love him, who have been called according to his purpose.

—Romans 8:28

Hope is a good and necessary thing. Expectation and anticipation help get us through difficult days. But life has a tendency to threaten to squash our hopes and sink our expectations. Maybe you thought you'd have lost twenty pounds by now, or perhaps you hoped you would have a different job. Is this a time of disappointment, or a time when your dreams are coming true?

Whether your days are filled with hopeful excitement, dashed dreams, or somewhere in between, take comfort in this fact: God knows where you came from, and He knows where you are going. He knows your past and your future; He knows your every hope and dream. Rather than hoping for and expecting great things of your life, why not hope for and expect great things of your great God? Rest in the certainty that He will never disappoint you.

Thank You for always coming through, Father, even when Your plans don't match up with my own.

Present Your Requests to God

Do not be anxious about anything, but in all things, by prayer and petition, with thanksgiving, present your requests to God.

—Philippians 4:6

When the Bible says to present your requests to God, it means to bring everything before Him—every request, no matter how big or small. Perhaps this means asking Him to heal your sick father or to help you get through the day without yelling at your kids. You could ask Him to lead you in your life's next step, or you might simply need His help to get through that meeting you're dreading. Whatever your requests are, lay them before God.

It's in our nature to feel strange about bringing some of our requests to the Lord, thinking they are too small in comparison to the world's great problems of poverty, injustice, and sin. But nothing is too small for the Lord. If you're withholding some of your requests from the Lord today, lay them down at His feet and then look up to your heavenly Father. He is ready to listen.

Dear Lord, help me remember that nothing is too big or too small to bring to You in prayer.

Perfect and Never-Ending Love

"I am the good shepherd. The good shepherd lays down his life for the sheep."

—John 10:11

You work. You work to earn money. You work to earn approval. You work to earn the respect of a boss and the trust of new acquaintances. You even work to earn love—from friends, from family, from a spouse. But there is one thing you never have to work for, never have to earn: the love of the Lord Jesus. His love is simply yours—because you are you, and because He longs for you to be His. It's that simple.

Yes, there are many things you can do to please the Lord, and He does want you to serve Him. But His love for you is freely given, and it is so vast and complete that He was willing to lay down His life for you. When you are overwhelmed and exhausted by working to earn the love and approval of those around you, remember the perfect and never-ending love of Christ—and rest in Him.

Thank You, Jesus, for giving up Your life so that I could freely and fully receive Your love.

Life Is Messy

I consider my life worth nothing to me; my only aim is to finish the race and complete the task the Lord Jesus has given me—the task of testifying to the good news of God's grace.

—Acts 20:24

Life is full of beautiful things: vibrant sunflowers, a perfect game, sunsets, bluebirds, and birch trees. And sometimes, it's tempting to show others only the beautiful things in our lives. To present the perfect picture, we push the clutter out of the way, suck in our stomachs, throw the dishes in the dishwasher, or stash the miscellaneous piles in the spare bedroom. We don't want others to know about the messy parts.

Yes, life is beautiful, but it's also messy. And we all have our own messes—our own secrets, dirty laundry, and less-than-perfect past. The good news is this: God can turn messy into beautiful. You don't have to have it all together. It's okay if your life is less than picture-perfect.

Rely on the Lord, and rest in Him. Don't hide your brokenness from Him—not only can He mend it, but He can also transform it into something beautiful.

Father, thank You for sending Jesus to turn my messy, sinful self into something beautiful.

Stop Withholding Rest

Grace and peace to you from God our Father and the Lord Jesus Christ.

—1 Corinthians 1:3

You may not realize it, but often *you're* the one withholding rest from yourself. It's shockingly easy to do. Whether you're working at an office, running a household, providing for a family, trying to provide for yourself, or all of the above, life gets busy. A lot rests on your shoulders, and you're afraid to set down even a part of that burden, aren't you?

But you don't have to carry it all or all alone or all the time. Trust in the One who is holding out His hands to you. Lay your worries and burdens down at the throne of God, and let Him shoulder your anxieties. The Lord will provide for you. Right now, you need to rest. You have permission. Do whatever it takes—time away from work or school, letting go of a few responsibilities, or asking for help. Rest is within your reach; let yourself have it.

Teach me to rest, Lord. I am tired and weary. Show me and correct me when I withhold rest from myself.

No Fear

To the person who pleases him, God gives wisdom, knowledge and happiness.

—Ecclesiastes 2:26

Have you ever suffered from a case of FOMO: Fear of Missing Out? It's a recently coined phrase, but it describes a fear we've all felt at one point or another. When we say no to an event or opportunity, we cringe to think of what we might be missing out on. So to ensure we don't miss out, we say yes to an awful lot—more than we probably should. And then we wonder why we're so burned out.

It's hard to say no. But it's a word that we need to become more comfortable saying. Saying no doesn't have to be unkind or thoughtless; it can be said with gentleness. And saying no can open up more space in our lives to say yes to the things that matter to us, such as time with the Lord.

So teach yourself to say no without fear. And then raise your hand in a triumphant yes!

When I say no, I'm afraid I'll miss out on something important. Show me, Lord, what is truly important.

On Struggles with Health

My son, pay attention to what I say; turn your ear to my words. Do not let them out of your sight, keep them within your heart; for they are life to those who find them and health to one's whole body.

—Proverbs 4:20–22

We all know someone struggling with health issues. Who has been on your heart recently? Maybe it's a child with leukemia, a neighbor with Parkinson's, or a best friend with chronic fatigue. This world has troubles, and our bodies are not immune to it; we are broken people with broken bodies.

Or perhaps you have perplexing health issues of your own. Maybe you've had rounds of tests with no easy answers, or treatments with no results. Health issues can be frightening because they expose how fragile we really are.

Whether you are wrestling with health issues or you know someone who is, it can be a scary, uncertain, and vulnerable time. Take comfort in the God who is above all things. He knows your fears and cares for you more than words can describe. Call out to Him when you feel anxious; He wants you to rest in His love, which can drive out all fear.

Lord, health issues are so scary. Please take away the fear and help me rest in Your never-ending love.

A Sabbath's Rest

The seventh day is a sabbath to the LORD your God. On it you shall not do any work, neither you, nor your son or daughter, nor your male or female servant, nor your animals, nor any foreigner residing in your towns.

—Exodus 20:10

What does your Sabbath day normally look like? Is it peaceful or full of activity? Do you end the day feeling rested, or filled with dread for the week ahead? Maybe your job doesn't allow you to enjoy a typical Sunday Sabbath, and you find yourself thinking of it as just another day.

God gave us a Sabbath—not because He needed to rest, but because we need to rest. God knew our weeks would be busy and our days full, and so He provided us with a reprieve from it all. The Sabbath is a day to rest, reflect on the Lord, and refuel for the next week. Yes, it's traditionally on Sunday, but if that isn't possible for you, any day of the week works.

Take time away from the daily hustle and bustle. Let your soul breathe and your shoulders relax. Let your heart sing of God's goodness for another week. *Rest.*

Lord, this Sabbath day, turn my eyes to You, Your goodness, and Your faithfulness, and help me to rest.

Coveting and Comparing

I have been crucified with Christ and I no longer live, but Christ lives in me. The life I now live in the body, I live by faith in the Son of God, who loved me and gave himself for me.

—Galatians 2:20

When the Lord gave us the Ten Commandments and included "Thou shalt not covet," He knew that we, as humans, were likely to fall into the trap of comparison and jealousy. It is incredibly easy to do—and at times, it feels harmless—but it robs us of gratitude for what we do have. We compare physical appearances, possessions, personalities, talents, and even spiritual lives. Comparison is a mind game, and we need to stop playing it.

Do you want freedom from the comparison trap? Try focusing on what you *have* rather than what you wish you had. Make a list of all that you're thankful for. Yes, it's elementary, but it's also practically foolproof. When your blessings are written out, right there in front of you, they're much more tangible, and you'll begin to see that you truly are blessed.

Take the first step in finding rest from comparison by beginning that list. You'll be amazed at how long it quickly becomes.

Father, thank You for my many blessings. Open my eyes to the beauty in my own life.

Whatever Is True

Finally, brothers and sisters, whatever is true, whatever is noble, whatever is right, whatever is pure, whatever is lovely, whatever is admirable—if anything is excellent or praiseworthy—think about such things.

—Philippians 4:8

Anger. Jealousy. Self-contempt. Annoyance. How often do you think negatively? If you're stuck in a traffic jam, is your mind full of frustration toward other drivers? When your spouse disagrees with a decision you made, do you let bitterness overtake you? Do you often find yourself thinking more negatively than positively throughout the day? If so, then perhaps it's time to change the way you think.

It's easy—all too easy—to wallow in self-pity or to fixate on your own anger or someone else's issues. But in doing so, you rob yourself of the joy found in all that is true, noble, right, pure, lovely, admirable, excellent, and praiseworthy. If your mind is a swirling realm of destructive thoughts, there's no room for anything else.

Today, focus instead on what is true—that you are blessed by a God who loves you. Give your mind and body a break from negativity, and rest in the goodness of God.

Father, guide my thoughts. Teach me to focus on whatever is pure and true.

Ease Up on Earning

Surely he took up our pain and bore our suffering, yet we considered him punished by God, stricken by him, and afflicted.

—Isaiah 53:4

You volunteer in several ministries, serve on committees, counsel others in times of need, and make yourself available for every service opportunity. Others look to you as an example, a servant of the Lord with a never-ending heart for service. But, in reality, you're tired. You crave a Sunday that involves more rest than work, and you really want a night to yourself.

Does this sound familiar, friend? If so, find freedom in this truth: you can't earn more of God's love by serving on more committees, and you can't serve everyone's needs without becoming needy yourself. Sometimes, you just need to ease up on earning everyone's approval.

Find time this week to simply sit in God's presence. Carve out an hour to be alone with Him and to rejuvenate. It's not lazy or self-serving; it's what is required to be an effective servant of the Lord. Let yourself rest.

I find myself trying to earn Your love, Jesus. Remind me that You love me just because I'm me.

Getting Over Overscheduling

You, LORD, hear the desire of the afflicted; you encourage them, and you listen to their cry.

—Psalm 10:17

You look at the calendar, and your heart sinks. Every night of the week is busy, and the weekend is crammed with activities, chores, and errands. We can all relate. Overscheduling is easy to do, and it's hard to know how to maintain a less hectic agenda. After all, the church needs you, your colleagues need you, your family needs you—and after saying yes to all their needs, there's little, if any, time left for you. Are you *over* overscheduling yourself?

It's true that we all have commitments we can't bail on, and some seasons of life are busier than others. When you're overwhelmed with overscheduling, turn to God. Give Him your schedule. Ask Him to sift through your calendar and reveal to you the things that can go and the things that should stay. Lean on Him and His strength. He will uphold you; He will help you; He will guide you to rest.

Lord, show me the activities I can let go of, and guide me to those things I should keep.

The Danger of a Crystal Ball

There is surely a future hope for you, and your hope will not be cut off.

—Proverbs 23:18

It would be nice to have a crystal ball, to know exactly what the future holds. That would take such a load of worry and fear off your shoulders, right? Or would it make you even more fearful?

Yes, there are surely exciting and wonderful things waiting for you in the future. But because we live in a sinful world, there will also be trials ahead. There will be scary and uncharted territory, pain, and confusion. And knowing the difficult things you'll one day face might be more than your heart can handle right now.

God understands your hopes and concerns for the future, but He also knows you can't handle it all at once. God will faithfully provide everything you need to walk with Him each day—He just asks that you trust Him, one day at a time. No, you can't know the future. But you can know and trust the One who does.

Father, You know my future and all its joys and pain. I trust You to guide me through it.

Truth Like Rain

The LORD your God is with you, the Mighty Warrior who saves. He will take great delight in you; in his love he will no longer rebuke you, but will rejoice over you with singing.

—Zephaniah 3:17

You are God's beloved. He rejoices over you with singing and watches over you while you sleep at night. He knit you together with His own hands, and He delights in you. When you choose to follow Him, He adopts you into His own family. His mercies are new every morning, and His faithfulness continues on and on forever.

Even now, Jesus is preparing a place for you in heaven. Because of His great and abiding love for you, He suffered, died, and rose again. And because of His sacrifice, you are able to approach God's throne with confidence and expectation.

When you read those words, let their truth fall on you like rain. Let their goodness penetrate your heart and saturate your soul. You are deeply loved by the One who formed the seas and carved the mountains. And He promises you rest from your weariness, reprieve from your worry, and forgiveness from your sins. What a gift!

Too often I forget what a gift Your love is, dear Lord. Thank You for loving me.

Moments That Matter

Be very careful, then, how you live—not as unwise but as wise, making the most of every opportunity.

—Ephesians 5:15–16

You tell yourself you'll do it later. Someday you'll learn to sew, catch up with an old friend, begin that project, take your mom to lunch, or plan a date with your spouse. *Someday.* You'll do it when you have more time and when it's more convenient. But why wait for someday? Why not do it today?

When work and chores and responsibilities crowd your life, a certain type of rest can come from doing the special things, the meaningful things. It's not irresponsible to take time away from the everyday to indulge your creative side, to nurture that relationship, or even to just plan and dream a little. These are the moments you'll most remember, and they're the ones—years from now—for which you'll be most grateful. So call your mom, take your dad to the game, reunite with an old friend, learn to bake. Rest in the moments that matter.

Lord, help me take time for the moments that truly matter in my life.

Making Time for Retreat

*I consider that our present sufferings are not worth comparing with
the glory that will be revealed in us.*

—Romans 8:18

Quiet. *Solitude. Sleep. Rejuvenation.* Even the words sound wonderful. You may be longing for deep, soul-quieting rest, but the daily demands of your life make it an unlikely dream. Take comfort in these promises from Isaiah: "The LORD is the everlasting God. . . . He will not grow tired or weary, and . . . those who hope in the LORD will renew their strength. They will soar on wings like eagles; they will run and not grow weary, they will walk and not be faint" (40:28, 31).

Not only does the Lord not grow tired or weary, but He also gives you strength when you are weary. Even if you can't escape the busyness of your life, you can still find rest for your soul. Take comfort in the Lord's words today, dear friend. He can give you retreat and reprieve—even in the midst of your rush-and-tumble day. Ask Him for it, and then thank Him for the answer you can believe is coming.

*Lord, I'm so grateful that You don't grow weary and that You
promise to give me strength.*

Good Morning

I will sing of your strength, in the morning I will sing of your love.
—Psalm 59:16

Morning. It's the time to get up, get ready, and begin your day. It's the starting point of the day. And it's also a wonderful time to rest. Yes, you did just wake up, and yes, you have a million things to do. But if you begin your day with a rested spirit, the remainder of your day will be more likely to be restful too.

Savor the morning. Take a moment to slowly breathe in and out. Yawn and stretch and open the curtains. Enjoy the sunrise. Sit with your Bible and your coffee and find respite and relief in the promises of your Lord. Let your mind be filled with joy for the day. Before the demands begin, before cars are started, traffic is jammed, and patience is running thin, enjoy these quiet moments of the morning.

Lord, let the quiet beauty of my morning carry me through the day.

Only a Prayer Away

Let us then approach God's throne of grace with confidence, so that
we may receive mercy and find grace to help us in our time of need.
—Hebrews 4:16

With today's technology, it's easy to stay connected with friends, family, current events, and even old classmates from elementary school. Just a few clicks and swipes, and relationships are easily established, nourished, and renewed.

But connecting with Jesus is even easier. There's no technology required, because He's only a simple prayer away. No cell service? No problem. You can connect with Jesus even in the middle of nowhere, or in the dead of night, or the middle of the afternoon. He never ignores your calls, and He never asks if He can get back with you later. God is available anytime and all the time.

Isn't that a relief? Isn't that an amazing promise? Jesus is there for you always, no matter the time or circumstance. He can give you the counsel, encouragement, and rest you so desperately need. Connect with Jesus today; He's only a prayer away.

Dear Jesus, thank You for never being too busy, tired, or
overwhelmed to hear my prayers.

Retreat at Home

He stilled the storm to a whisper; the waves of the sea were hushed.
They were glad when it grew calm, and he guided them to their
desired haven.

—Psalm 107:29–30

When you think of the word *retreat*, you probably don't think of your own home with its piles of laundry, fix-it list, and cluttered countertops. Instead, visions of white, sandy beaches or rustic mountain cabins probably fill your thoughts. After all, a retreat should be a break away from the demands of ordinary, everyday life, right?

Often, we don't have the time or money to go on a far-away retreat. So have you ever thought of letting your home be your destination for retreat?

Even if you simply designate one spot—your bedroom, backyard, or a quiet corner—to be your haven, it can be made restful. Clear away the clutter and banish distractions. Add a candle, a painting, green plants, or your favorite chair. And then . . . retreat. Take a nap, listen to calming music, read your Bible, and revel in your haven. Allow yourself to rest deeply—for a moment, for an hour, for an afternoon.

Heavenly Father, bless me with extraordinary rest in my ordinary haven.

Peace from Within

You are my strength, I sing praise to you; you, God, are my fortress, my God on whom I can rely.

—Psalm 59:17

Have you ever met anyone who had an unbelievably crazy-busy schedule, but instead of being stressed and fatigued, that person exuded a peaceful calm and an utter reliance on Jesus? That's called *inner rest*. It's a peace that depends not upon circumstances, personality, or even organization; instead, it comes from a prayerful spirit and an intentional dependence on the Lord.

With inner rest, your life may look hectic on the outside, and you may not get as much sleep as you wish each night, but your daily, hourly, and sometimes minute-by-minute surrendering to the Lord keeps your spirit firmly planted in peace instead of despair.

Dear friend, do you need internal rest today? It's available to you. Ask the Lord to lead you to true, deep, inner rest, to the peace and calm that can only come from Him. Ask, and He will give you rest.

Oh God, I deeply desire inner rest. Please help me surrender my life completely to You.

Finding Strength in Rest

Strengthen the feeble hands, steady the knees that give way; say to those with fearful hearts, "Be strong, do not fear; your God will come."

—Isaiah 35:3–4

There are those rare individuals who thrive on just three hours of sleep, but most of us need more. And when we don't get enough rest, we slowly begin dropping—one by one—all those balls we've been juggling. Our time with God, our time with family and friends, our work, and other interests begin to suffer, and it's not a good feeling.

If you think resting is a sign of weakness, think again. Those who are strong give themselves the rest they need. Even the most perfect man who walked the earth—Jesus—recognized when His human body needed rest, and He took time for it. Rest doesn't make you weak; it makes you strong.

So let yourself rest so you can perform well in your job, so you can be present with your family and friends, and so you can be dependable and strong for those who need you.

Lord, You've filled my life with wonderful people. Help me rest so I can better love them.

Living in Love

We know and rely on the love God has for us. God is love. Whoever lives in love lives in God, and God in them.

—1 John 4:16

If someone has wronged you, you may still feel the pain, even if it happened years ago. A harsh comment, broken trust, a stab in the back—everyone has experienced some sort of hurt in his or her life. But if you're still holding on to that bitterness, pain, shame, or desire for revenge, it's time to let go. And in letting go, you will find freedom, peace, and rest.

First John 4:16 reminds us of how we are to live even amid the hurts and sorrows of this world: we are to live in love. Notice that God's Word doesn't say we are to live in love *unless* we've been hurt. No, we are to live in love, period.

As this truth sinks in, ask your Savior to show you how to let go of past hurts. Beseech Him to replace them with His love, joy, peace, kindness, and hope. For Christ can heal even the deepest wound and bless you with rest for your soul.

Help me live in love, dear Jesus, especially when I've been wronged.

When Hopes Are Dashed

As you do not know the path of the wind, or how the body is formed in a mother's womb, so you cannot understand the work of God, the Maker of all things.

—Ecclesiastes 11:5

As children, we have big dreams for the future. As we grow up, enter high school, go to college or get a job, and watch the years pass by, our lives can branch out in countless directions. Some of those childhood dreams come true, but others do not.

Does your life look completely different than you thought it would? Maybe you'd hoped to have a child or dreamed of being married, but it just hasn't happened. Perhaps the career you worked so hard for just isn't fulfilling. Or retirement isn't what you'd hoped. Life is hard—especially when hopes and dreams are dashed.

If you feel this way, look to the Lord. He understands your frustrations and disappointments. And more than anything, He wants you to confide in Him and trust Him to lead you. God can transform those dashed hopes into part of His amazing plan—and you can rest in fulfilling His purpose for your life.

Oh, Lord my God, I place my hopes and dreams in Your steady and loving hands.

Incorporate Life-Giving Activities

Whatever your hand finds to do, do it with all your might.

—Ecclesiastes 9:10

If you had a week to do absolutely anything you love, what would it include? For some, gardening ranks at the top of the list. For others, it's heading to the lake to fish. Or perhaps hiking, reading, spending time with friends, spending time alone, or going to a museum makes you smile.

These are things that give you life. They're not the mundane "I have time so I might as well clean out the garage" activities (though that does bring joy to some). These are the things that bring you joy and leave you feeling refreshed and fulfilled.

Incorporate one of your favorite activities into your week. Maybe you can't go fishing for a whole week, but how about an afternoon? Browse through a gardening magazine at lunch or slip over to a museum after work. Giving yourself even small doses of these life-giving activities will bring you soothing rest.

Lord, show me ways to incorporate the things I love into my everyday life.

When Your Body Says No

I praise you because I am fearfully and wonderfully made; your works are wonderful, I know that full well.

—Psalm 139:14

God created each of us to be unique and wonderful. Our bodies are masterpieces, and they're designed to tell us when we're hungry, happy, sad, anxious, sick, or excited. They also tell us when we're tired.

When we are weary and exhausted, it shows physically. Dark circles appear under our eyes, our eyes sting with strain, our limbs feel sluggish, and our hearts sink when the alarm clock blares. Sound familiar?

When your body is telling you it's tired, what do you do? Do you try to push through and keep going until you reach your breaking point? Or perhaps you ignore the symptoms until you get physically sick. We live in a culture that glorifies busyness, but at some point, you really need to rest. Honor your body when it signals its tiredness. You are fearfully and wonderfully made. Respect your body and give yourself the rest you deserve.

You created our bodies so intricately, Father. Help me honor Your creation with rest.

Get Outside

Let all creation rejoice before the LORD, for he comes, he comes to judge the earth. He will judge the world in righteousness and the peoples in his faithfulness.

—Psalm 96:13

In today's world, children are spending more and more time inside, while experts are encouraging parents to take their kids outside. Why? Because being outside in nature helps children not just physically, but also mentally and socially. It boosts their intellect, immune system, and emotional well-being. It's just a good thing to do.

And it's not just good for children; it's good for you too. Can you find time today to go outside? Take a bike ride, or get your heart rate up with a walk. Find a pool to splash in, walk by the lake, or explore a hiking trail. You'll be refreshed in a way that only the majesty of God's creation can provide. The combination of trees, fresh air, sunshine, wind, water, physical movement, the smell of dirt, and the beauty of bright blooms is healing in a unique way that nothing else is. So open the door and step outside . . . to rest.

The beauty of Your world amazes me, Father God. Refresh me with Your creation.

Time to Wait

The creation waits in eager expectation for the children of God to be revealed.

—Romans 8:19

As a child, you often had to wait. Wait for the cookies to come out of the oven, wait your turn, wait until your dad was off the phone, or wait for permission to watch TV. Now that you're grown up, you're able to bypass waiting in many ways. If you want ice cream, you drive to the store. If you want to watch a movie, you turn on the television. You try to eliminate waiting as much as possible. But there can be good in waiting.

Waiting builds character. It teaches patience and reliance on God. If you're waiting for something—a spouse, a new job, retirement, or the salvation of a friend—find rest in the waiting. Trust in the Lord's perfect provision and perfect timing. Let the waiting carve compassion into your heart and draw you nearer to God as He draws even nearer to you. Remember, the Lord is close to those who wait upon His will.

I'm not great at waiting, Jesus. Help my waiting to be a time of hope, not despair.

The Balancing Act

When you lie down, you will not be afraid; when you lie down,
your sleep will be sweet.

—Proverbs 3:24

Work-life balance is a hot topic, isn't it? Working moms and dads, young professionals, older adults, CEOs, interns, and many others are seeking answers for how to live a balanced life. You want to do good work at your job— whether that's at an office, at home with kids, at church, or at school—but you also want to have a healthy home life. You want to find a balance between rest and work, but the solutions are eluding you.

If you're struggling to figure out the balancing act, turn to the Lord. He knows how to help you achieve true and restful balance in your life. He created you for work, but He also created you for Sabbath and rest. Ask Him to lead you to a balanced life, and trust Him to watch over your world while you rest.

Dear Lord, I need more balance in my life. Please open my eyes to
opportunities for rest.

SEPTEMBER

"In repentance and rest is your salvation,
in quietness and trust is your strength."

—Isaiah 30:15

Peace in Every Way

May the Lord of peace himself give you peace at all times and in every way.

—2 Thessalonians 3:16

"Peace at all times and in every way"—that is God's gift to His children. But how? How does He give you this peace?

First, it is found through His Word, through the stories, poems, and truths that illustrate His timeless love and care for those who follow Him.

Second, God gives peace through His promises: promises to never leave or forsake you, to deliver you in times of trouble, to take away your burdens, and to give you rest. There is peace to be found in His promises of grace to cover all our sins and to provide for every need.

And then peace is also found in the people God places in your life. Other believers can speak truth to your heart, pray with you, journey with you, and point you toward Christ.

Open yourself up to the God who loves you and allow Him to radically flood your life with peace at all times, in every way.

Father, flood me with Your peace, at all times and in every way.

Dimming the Noise

The LORD is in his holy temple; let all the earth be silent before him.
—Habakkuk 2:20

Finding a quiet place may sound simple to do, but it rarely is in this noise-filled world. It's incredibly easy to get caught up in the hustle, bustle, speed, and anxiety of life. Sitting in a quiet place to rest for a bit almost feels . . . wasteful and decadent. But, dear friend, that's just what you need to do.

Dimming the noise and tuning out everything except the voice of your heavenly Father is crucial. Sitting with Him in the morning, at the end of the day, or any time at all will calm your soul. Just a few moments of silence in His presence will help refocus your eyes and heart on Him instead of on yourself and your own strength. Let His voice speak over any troubles you have in your life, and allow the quiet power of His Word to penetrate your life. Let God give you rest.

Father, help me tune out the noise of the world and focus on You.

Be Gentle with Yourself

For to us a child is born, to us a son is given, and the government will be on his shoulders. And he will be called Wonderful Counselor, Mighty God, Everlasting Father, Prince of Peace.

—Isaiah 9:6

You think about last night, and you shake your head. There was so much you wanted to get done, but instead you fell asleep on the couch, completely exhausted. And that already huge to-do list? It only got longer.

Friend, be gentle with yourself. If you are weary, you need to rest. If you're juggling too many commitments, you need to toss a few to someone else. If you're falling behind in life's demands, you may be expecting too much of yourself. Be gentle, *exceedingly gentle*, with your tired body and mind.

When Jesus called the weary and heavy laden to Himself, He didn't berate or lecture them. Instead, He welcomed them, and He promised to carry their load. Why not give the Savior your heavy load? Hear His words of love and grace instead of your own words of negativity and condemnation. Find rest in the Prince of Peace.

Dear loving Savior, please take this heavy load and fill me with peaceful rest.

The Work of the Cross

LORD, you establish peace for us; all that we have accomplished you have done for us.

—Isaiah 26:12

When Jesus said from the cross, "It is finished," He paid the price for your sin once and for all (John 19:30). He gave His life, the ultimate sacrifice, so that you wouldn't have to bear the punishment. Are you living in the freedom of that?

Too many Christians are still trying to earn God's favor by living perfectly. But that's impossible; and, thankfully, God doesn't call you to be perfect. Instead, He calls you to trust Him completely and to believe in the finished work of the cross.

Can you allow yourself to rest in the work of the cross today? Can you let go of the urge to continually prove yourself and your faithfulness to God? Today, surrender your quest for perfection, and simply praise God for what He's done for you. Let your life be marked by complete reliance on the work of the cross. Rest in the peace of your salvation.

Jesus, Lamb of God, thank You for paying the price for my sin. I rest in that peace.

Armed with Rest

"Though the mountains be shaken and the hills be removed, yet my unfailing love for you will not be shaken nor my covenant of peace be removed," says the LORD, who has compassion on you.

—Isaiah 54:10

Picture a knight in shining armor. He has a breastplate, chainmail, and a helmet. His entire body is protected, and because of his armor, the blows of battle are deflected. You too can fit yourself with basic armor in your daily life. It isn't made of metal, and it's not heavy to wear, but it can protect you in so many ways. That armor is called *rest*. Yes, rest.

When you are rested, you can better control your emotions and reactions. With rest, your decisions are more thoughtful, and your body is strengthened. You are more patient and kind, healthy and energized, and less susceptible to attack—both physically and spiritually. Rest, then, is an important part of your armor in this battle of life.

But how often do you put on the armor of rest? It may seem insubstantial and unimportant, but it is truly a powerful defensive weapon. Put on the armor of rest today.

Lord, remind me to arm myself with rest so that I will be ready for the battle of life.

Loving the Unlovable

Dear friends, let us love one another, for love comes from God.
Everyone who loves has been born of God and knows God.
Whoever does not love does not know God, because God is love.

—1 John 4:7–8

Loving those who are lovable is easy. But loving our enemies? Well, that's another story.

A friend who hurt you deeply, that person who betrayed your trust—these are the people who are hard to love. Yet, when Jesus was on the cross, that's exactly what He did. Even as His enemies jeered, Jesus prayed, "Father, forgive them, for they do not know what they are doing" (Luke 23:34). He loved the unlovable.

Jesus' example and His extravagant love make it possible for us to love others, even those who've hurt us. Because of His sacrifice, we can claim the supernatural strength to take a deep breath, rest our head on the Father's chest, and say, "I will love my enemies." If you're carrying a burden of anger or resentment, put it down and rest in the Lord's power to help you love even the unlovable.

Heavenly Father, help me love my enemies. I can only do it through Your strength.

Wise Rest

Teach us to use wisely all the time we have.

—Psalm 90:12 CEV

A time of rest can easily and quickly become a time of unrest. Perhaps you've just settled in for your early morning quiet time, but as you try to pray your mind begins to wander to all you need to do in the day. Or maybe you've carved out an hour to simply sit and enjoy the stillness, but you soon realize you've spent half the time scrolling through your social media updates.

Are you using your times of rest wisely? There's no set right or wrong way to rest; it can be sleep or activity, it can be indoors or outdoors. But however you choose to rest, it should provide you with energy, joy, and peace. You should leave your time of rest feeling rejuvenated and relieved of your weariness. And if you don't, you might need to make some changes. Whatever type of rest you choose, do it intentionally and wisely.

Father, may my time of rest be pleasing to You and beneficial to me.

God Is Bigger

We are hard pressed on every side, but not crushed; perplexed, but not in despair; persecuted, but not abandoned; struck down, but not destroyed.

—2 Corinthians 4:8–9

Before Jesus left this earth, He said, "In this world you will have trouble. But take heart! I have overcome the world" (John 16:33). Jesus states a fact: we will have trouble. Life will be hard. So if you're feeling as if life is just one battle after another, that doesn't surprise Jesus. He predicted it for His disciples thousands of years ago and it's still true for His followers today. But Jesus didn't leave us to wallow in that trouble; instead, He gave us hope.

We have hope because, through His death and resurrection, He has already overcome the world. We don't need to worry, fear, or despair. We know how the story will end— with Jesus' complete victory!

If you are weakening under a heavy load of troubles, take heart because the Lord is stronger. He is bigger. He is your Deliverer and Provider, and He can give you rest from despair.

Jesus, I cling to You and to Your words of encouragement. Thank You for being my refuge.

Why Rest?

Every athlete exercises self-control in all things.

—1 Corinthians 9:25 ESV

If you've ever watched interviews of Olympic athletes or read an article about their training regimen, you've noticed that they all have something in common, whether they're gymnasts, sprinters, or speed skaters. They all allow their bodies to rest.

God didn't create our bodies to be in continual motion. Resting allows the body time to repair its muscles and strengthen itself. That's true if you're an Olympic runner or if you can barely jog around the block.

So . . . have you been letting yourself rest? Yes, your life is full of demands, from cooking and cleaning to raising children, from running for student body president to running a company, and everything in between. The demands of life put stress on your body, mind, and spirit—and rest is the best way to prevent a breakdown. Take a tip from some Olympic athletes: work hard, and then allow yourself time to rest.

Father, I push my body too hard sometimes. Help me slow down and rest.

Desire into Action

Earnestly desire the higher gifts. And I will show you a still more excellent way.

—1 Corinthians 12:31 ESV

When babies are learning to walk, they begin by taking one tiny, tentative step forward. As they become more comfortable, they start taking more and more steps until, *voilà*, they're toddling. It takes lots of practice, and a few bumps and bruises along the way are inevitable.

The same could be said of cultivating a life of rest. You may desire rest, but you won't find it until you take that first tiny, tentative step toward it. It will take lots of practice before rest becomes an integral part of your life. And yes, there'll be a few bumps and bruises along the way.

But don't be discouraged. Taking small steps, falling down, and getting back up are part of the learning process. So take a small step toward rest today. Say no to an extra responsibility. Ask for help. Adjust your priorities. It may feel wobbly and strange, but that's okay. You're learning to rest.

Lord, hold my hand and encourage me as I take the next step toward rest.

Finding Courage

Trust in the LORD with all your heart and lean not on your own understanding; in all your ways submit to him, and he will make your paths straight.

—Proverbs 3:5–6

True rest takes courage. It takes deep trust to release control and surrender to God's plans. Because even when we're exhausted, we still like to feel that we're in control. To turn over our plans, work, and productivity to the Lord and to rest in Him—that requires a huge leap of faith. Yes, it takes courage to rest.

Do you want that courage? Are you simply so tired that you don't even know where to turn? Rest assured, friend, that the Lord is trustworthy. Turn to Him. He holds the whole world in His hands, and yet He also knows every hair on your head. He is deeply and intrinsically involved in your life, and He wants to free you from exhaustion and give you a spirit of rest.

When you surrender yourself to the Lord, you can know that your loving Father will take care of you. Ask Him for the courage to surrender; ask Him for the courage to rest.

Lord, I am tired. I am weary. Please take control, and give me courage to let go.

The Harm of Complaining

Don't grumble against one another, brothers and sisters, or you will be judged. The Judge is standing at the door!

—James 5:9

Sometimes complaining feels good, doesn't it? At least for a few minutes. But then you usually end up feeling even more frustrated, jaded, or angry than before. Complaining doesn't help you forget or move on; it solidifies your feelings of being wronged. And those feelings can begin to take root deep down inside you, hardening your heart.

Where there is complaining, there is no peace. Peace comes from a contented heart, from understanding that life isn't fair, and from choosing to embrace what life has to offer you. Peace is a restful state. Complaining, on the other hand, brings only weariness.

The next time you find yourself complaining, note how your body reacts. You may feel your blood pressure rise, shoulders tighten, and hands curl into fists. This isn't healthy or restful. Let go of your complaints, turn them over to God in prayer, and let Him replace them with peace and contentment . . . and rest.

Lord, please take this complaining spirit of mine and replace it with peaceful trust in You.

No Safer Place

You know the message God sent to the people of Israel, announcing the good news of peace through Jesus Christ, who is Lord of all.

—Acts 10:36

The story of Jesus and His disciples caught out at sea in a storm is well known. But have you ever thought of applying that story to your own struggle for rest? Most often, we focus on Jesus' power in that story—how His simple words calmed a deadly storm. But notice what happens before He spoke: the disciples went to Jesus.

You see, the disciples were on a boat, caught in a horrendous storm. It was a matter of life or death. So what did they do? *They turned to Jesus*. Was their faith perfect? No. Were they still afraid? Yes. Did they doubt Him? Yes. But still they went to Him—and Jesus saved them.

Beloved, are you hurrying to Jesus when you're caught in the middle of a storm? There's no safer place. Believe in His power and strength; rest in His goodness and love. He won't let you drown.

Father, may I rest in You—especially when the storms in my life are threatening.

Lending a Hand

Carry each other's burdens, and in this way you will fulfill the law of Christ.

—Galatians 6:2

If you are in a season of feeling rested, it may be time for you to help others find rest. Look around at the loved ones in your life. Are any of them struggling? New moms and dads could always use a helping hand; anyone with health issues would surely love some assistance; a single parent would probably be overjoyed to have someone watch the kids for a bit.

As you think back on more hectic times in your own life, let those memories make you sensitive to those around you. This may be the time for the bad times to pay dividends in sympathy, life-tested solutions, and the much-needed gift of an "I've been there" for someone who is struggling.

Rest is so needed, but so elusive for many. How can you help make rest a reality for someone else? Make a plan and reach out to someone today.

Father, open my eyes to the needs of those around me.

Rest in Blessings

Surely you have granted him unending blessings and made him glad with the joy of your presence.

—Psalm 21:6

Take a moment to think of the many blessings in your life. Perhaps you'll think of things like health, loving parents, a warm bed, a clean bathroom, a hot shower, a steady job, a cup of coffee on a dreary day, friends who care, a lovely garden, a lawnmower, a running car—the list could go on and on and on. As you open your eyes to the blessings around you, the awareness is life-changing. And as you intentionally look for what God has given you, you'll continue to see more and more and still more blessings.

Now, imagine that every blessing is a feather. As they begin to heap up, one upon the other, they create an inviting place to rest. Yes, there are areas of your life that aren't so pleasant, and you may even feel the void of unanswered prayers. But for today, rest in your blessings, knowing that the Lord truly takes care of you.

Lord, help me to see my many blessings as wonderful proof that You keep Your promises.

In the Beginning

The LORD is my strength and my defense; he has become my salvation. He is my God, and I will praise him, my father's God, and I will exalt him.

—Exodus 15:2

The beginning of the week is often challenging. You're struggling to get back into the everyday routine, and the demands of work or home life—or both—are exactly that: demanding. So if you already feel a little worn out, don't be discouraged!

Give yourself a few moments alone today. Sit in the quiet and remind yourself of these truths: God is with you and for you. He will never leave or forsake you. He rejoices over you with singing. He loves you. He gives strength to the weary. He wants to lift your burdens from you. And He tells you to rest.

Breathe in these promises from God, and let the hope they provide soak into your heart. Ask the Lord to make them clear to you throughout your week. Yes, the days may still be busy, and at times you might feel overwhelmed, but the Lord is on your side. Rest in the comfort of that truth today.

Lord, speak Your truth into my life and throughout my days this week.

A Slower Pace

Glory to God in the highest heaven, and on earth peace to those on whom his favor rests.

—Luke 2:14

If you've ever been to a big city, such as Chicago or New York, you know that walking down the sidewalks and streets isn't a meandering stroll. The pace is fast—*really fast*. People are intent on getting to their destinations. That's a stark contrast to the pace of visitors at, say, the zoo. There, you pause every few feet to look at the zebras, lions, or bears. You wouldn't think of rushing through the zoo because you'd miss so much.

So consider this: as you go through your week, do you rush through the days like a city commuter, or do you pause to see what's truly happening around you?

Today, remember to slow down once in a while. Look around and notice your colleague's good work or your child's laughter. Pause to see the fluttering leaves and to look people in the eyes when you speak. Try a slower—more restful—approach to your week.

Help me remember that life isn't a race, Lord, and that You want my attention too.

Resting in Anticipation

"I give you peace, the kind of peace that only I can give. It isn't like the peace that this world can give. So don't be worried or afraid."

—John 14:27 CEV

When will it happen? How will this end? Is it almost over? When we're stuck in a time of waiting, we ask these questions over and over again. We want to know how much longer we'll be in this place and how our story will unfold. And it feels as if the waiting would be easier if we just knew the basic blueprint. Then we'd know how to prepare ourselves—whether we'll need to buck up and push through, steel ourselves for disappointment, walk away, or celebrate. But the Lord knows that even the basic blueprint would overwhelm us. So He calls us to trust.

God wants you to trust Him wholeheartedly and without reservation. How can you do that? By believing that He is a good and gracious God, that He is perfect and loving, and that you are His beloved child for whom He only has good plans. Rest in His goodness; rest in His plans.

Lord God, I surrender my plans and questions and ask that You teach me to trust You.

Good News

Send me your light and your faithful care, let them lead me.
—Psalm 43:3

It's the dreaded call: your blood tests came back abnormal and you need to go in for more tests. As you wait for the results, worry knots in your stomach. You feel overwhelmed and underprepared. Your mind races through all the possible scenarios—and most of them are bleak. At last, when the doctor calls, she says, "Everything is fine. No need to worry." Your shoulders sag in relief, the fear evaporates, and you're filled with gratitude.

God's Word is like that doctor's call. The Lord can see the trouble in this world, and He doesn't shy away from sharing stories of sin and evil and fear—but He also shares good news, and it is *eternally* good news. If you feel anxious and fearful, exhausted and strained, open up the Bible. Drink in His words of promised peace and joy. Let His words give you encouragement and hope. Let His words give you rest.

Thank You for Your holy Word, Father. It is like medicine for my soul.

Letting Others In

"You shall not make for yourself an image in the form of anything in heaven above or on the earth beneath or in the waters below."

—Exodus 20:4

If you are trying to keep others impressed with your job, home, family life, possessions, and all those other aspects of your life, it's not doing you—or anyone else—any good. And, chances are, you're more than a little tired. It's time to give others a key to the door of your real life.

Letting others into the messy, raw, frustrating, and joyful parts of your life is the most authentic thing you can do. And authenticity brings freedom. It bypasses the superficial and allows friendships to grow and respect to deepen. Being honest about both the good and bad in life loosens your hold on that picture-perfect, squeaky-clean—and oh so phony—image. Instead, you can simply be yourself.

Are you keeping others locked outside of your real life? Take a chance and let them in. You'll be amazed by your ability to share more easily and to rest more fully.

Forgive me for wanting others to think my life is perfect, Lord. Help me instead to be open and honest.

Questions Without Answers

According to his promise we are waiting for new heavens and a new earth in which righteousness dwells.

—2 Peter 3:13 ESV

The Internet is a massive part of our lives today. It gives us answers—like the location of the nearest Italian restaurant or the name of the twenty-second US president. It provides directions, health information, and recipes. And it does it all in less than a second.

But there are questions even the Internet cannot answer. *Who will I marry? Will my cancer come back? Is my son ever going to speak to me again? Will I get this job? Does she actually love me?*

Are you wrestling with unanswered questions? Do you wish God would just write the answer on the sky or appear in a burning bush? Talk to Him about it. Tell Him your worries, and confess your fears. Then, ask the Lord to give you peace about these unanswered questions, because, unlike the Internet, God cares for you. Rest in that truth.

Lord, You know my future, and even now You're directing my path. I will wait on You.

A Season of Rest

Sow righteousness for yourselves, reap the fruit of unfailing love,
and break up your unplowed ground; for it is time to seek the LORD,
until he comes and showers his righteousness on you.

—Hosea 10:12

Autumn is arriving. Depending on where you live, the leaves are changing colors, temperatures are dropping, evenings are filled with the scent of bonfires, and fields are bursting with pumpkins. The changing of the seasons is a wonderful reminder for us to rest.

As Ecclesiastes notes, there is a time and a season for all things. Strawberry plants bloom in spring, roses open their buds in summer, and fall is the time trees shed their leaves and all of nature prepares for winter's rest.

Maybe you are in a season of producing. Your schedule is busy, and you're growing weary. Remember, there will be an end to this season, and sometimes you may need to help it along. Don't live year-round in the summer of busyness. Give yourself the slowing down of fall; prepare yourself for a season of rest.

Lord, give me the wisdom to know when it is time for a season
of rest.

Resisting Stress

Say to those who have an anxious heart, "Be strong; fear not!"
—Isaiah 35:4 ESV

How often do you hear someone say, "I'm stressed"? Stress is interwoven in our modern lives. Yet, the havoc it plays on our bodies is frightening: heart disease, depression, digestive issues, autoimmune disorders, memory problems, and nervous habits are all effects of stress.

How can you combat stress in your life? It will take some effort. Try engaging your body in a physical activity like stretching, see a counselor, clear your calendar, and immerse yourself in prayer. Less busyness, more deep breathing, and fewer burdens will all lead to a life marked less by stress and more by rest.

But first and always, when you need help resisting stress, turn to the One who loves you best. Sit in the presence of the Most High God, and let Him lift away the tension in your body as you pray to Him. He can and will help you resist stress—and find rest.

I praise You, my King and my Maker, for You know—and You provide—exactly what I need.

Structuring a Rest-Filled Week

"And which of you by being anxious can add a single hour to his span of life?"

—Matthew 6:27 ESV

The days have a tendency to fly by, leaving you out of breath and out of energy, and you're not sure how to change your situation. Have you ever considered structuring your week so it's more conducive to rest?

Make a schedule at the beginning of the week and fill in all of your must-do items. As you list them, ask yourself if any of the items can be shared or altered. Can you figure out a carpool for your kids? Can you share meal preparation with a spouse or a friend? Can you better use the alone-time you do have—during your commute, early in the morning, or on your lunch break?

After seeing the structure of your week, you may be able to tweak it and allow yourself a time of rest every day. A rest-filled week won't simply fall into your waiting arms; it takes discipline and planning, but it will be worth it.

You, Lord, are a God of order. Help me bring order and rest to my life this week.

Find Contentment in Your Story

O Lord, you are my God; I will exalt you; I will praise your name, for you have done wonderful things, plans formed of old, faithful and sure.

—Isaiah 25:1 ESV

God is writing a story in each of our lives. Some stories are more dramatic than others. Maybe you grew up in a Christian home with two loving parents, or perhaps your parents divorced, leaving you dazed and wounded. Perhaps you endured a difficult childhood, are battling anxiety, or experienced a radical transformation that brought you to Christ.

Everyone's story is different, and everyone's story is beautiful. Don't ever feel ashamed of yours. Beloved child of God, the Lord of all creation is the Author of your story, and it is a reflection of His handiwork in your life. Each and every story is one of redemption and beauty.

Your story has the potential to touch others' lives—whether it's full of drama or full of peace. Revel in the fact that God is continuing to pen your story, shaping it into a masterpiece. And because Jesus came, you know it will have a happy ending.

Thank You for authoring my story, God. I find great peace in knowing You are holding the pen.

To Buy or Not to Buy?

Please accept my blessing that is brought to you, because God has dealt graciously with me, and because I have enough.

—Genesis 33:11 ESV

One of the easiest lies to believe is this: more stuff will make you happier. It's not a sin to go shopping, to buy a new car, a house, an oven, or a set of golf clubs. But if you're trying to purchase happiness and contentment, then what you are really buying is the lie.

There is nothing in this world that can perfectly satisfy. You could own a private villa in Italy, have a getaway house in the Caribbean, drive the latest model Porsche, and buy a new wardrobe every season, but without Christ, you'll never be perfectly satisfied. Only Jesus can fill the emptiness in your heart. Only He gives true contentment and joy. So if you're wondering whether to buy or not to buy, remind yourself that true contentment cannot be purchased. It can only be found in Christ. Only He will satisfy.

You are all I truly need, Jesus. Change me until You are all I want.

A Pattern of Rest

As obedient children, do not be conformed to the passions of your former ignorance.

—1 Peter 1:14 ESV

Romans 12:2 says, "Do not conform to the pattern of this world, but be transformed by the renewing of your mind. Then you will be able to test and approve what God's will is—his good, pleasing and perfect will." One of the patterns of our world is the pattern of busyness. The word *busy* comes out of our mouths more times than we realize, and for some of us, we can't imagine life not being busy.

So when we are commanded to "not conform to the pattern of this world," it's for our own good. God wants us, instead, to conform to His example. And if you think back to the Old Testament, one example He gave—and commanded us to follow—was the weekly ritual of rest.

Are you conforming to the world's pattern of busyness, or are you conforming to God's pattern of rest? Take the words of this verse to heart, and repeat them to yourself throughout the week as you seek to rest.

I love how Your Word speaks truth to me and guides me in my life, Father God.

Grace Alone
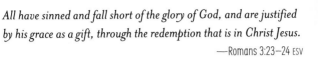

*All have sinned and fall short of the glory of God, and are justified
by his grace as a gift, through the redemption that is in Christ Jesus.*
—Romans 3:23–24 ESV

Ephesians 2:8 says, "It is by grace you have been saved,
through faith—and this is not from yourselves, it is the
gift of God." Did you see that, dear reader? You are not
saved through your own works. God isn't counting the
number of times you do something good, waiting for you
to reach a magic number that equals salvation. He isn't
looking at you to save yourself; salvation is His gift.

You are saved by grace, and it is only by grace that you
can come before the Lord in thanksgiving, sadness, and
doubt. It is only because of God's grace that you can have
eternal life. It has nothing to do with what you do, and
everything to do with what Christ did.

Isn't that a life-changing gift? We can rest in the salvation of Christ. We do not have to work for God's love;
it is already ours. Praise the Lord, for He has done good
things for us!

*Your grace brings me to my knees and humbles me. Thank You,
Lord, thank You!*

The Fruit of the Spirit

The fruit of the Spirit is love, joy, peace, patience, kindness, goodness, faithfulness, gentleness, self-control.

—Galatians 5:22–23 ESV

Can you recite the fruit of the Spirit? You may know them—love, joy, peace, patience, kindness, goodness, faithfulness, gentleness, and self-control—but can you still exemplify them when you're exhausted and worn down? Do you show gentleness and self-control when you're running on four hours of sleep? Are you able to be patient when you come home after working twelve hours straight and your children are fighting? Knowing the fruit of the Spirit is easy; living it is not.

When you are overwhelmed and overworked, and you aren't making time to sit in God's presence, other attributes rise up, such as impatience, anger, jealousy, and selfishness. But when your body and mind are rested, and when you are immersing yourself in the words of God, the fruit of the Spirit springs forth much more easily.

Take a few quiet moments to read through the fruit of the Spirit, and ask God to help you better live these things out in your life.

Fill me with Your Spirit, Lord, so that I can bear much fruit.

Steal, Kill, and Destroy

"The Son of Man came to seek and to save the lost."

—Luke 19:10

The Bible describes Satan as someone who comes to steal, kill, and destroy (John 10:10). If you have joy, he wants to replace it with sadness. If you are praising the Lord, he wants you to curse Him. If you are resting in quiet and peace, he wants to fill your life with noise and busyness. Satan is out to get you—and he's not playing nice.

Remember that when you sit down to talk to the Lord. You spend time with the Lord to get to know Him better and to grow your relationship with Him, but time spent with the Lord is also essential when fighting the Enemy. If you're daily reminding yourself of God's truth, it will be easier to recognize the wolf in sheep's clothing.

Guard your heart against the Enemy. Rest in the Lord's strong and comforting presence today, remembering that He came to seek and to save.

Protect me from the evil one, dear Father, as I rest in Your strength today.

OCTOBER

Oh, that I had the wings of a dove!
I would fly away and be at rest.

—Psalm 55:6

Autumn Rest

On the glorious splendor of Your majesty and on Your wonderful works, I will meditate.

—Psalm 145:5 NASB

Autumn is a unique season. With its dropping temperatures comes a rush of candy corn, pumpkins, shortening days, golden leaves, and the tiniest whisper of winter. Children jump in piles of leaves, and scarves are taken out of storage. Autumn's arrival means school is in session, early morning wake-up calls are in full swing, and it's more than acceptable to wear shorts *and* a sweater.

It's an absolutely beautiful time of the year. As your home gets cozier and you begin spending more time indoors, make sure you are enjoying some autumn rest. Grab some apple cider and spend some time in front of a fire. Settle in with a book and a blanket. Take a walk in the crisp autumn air, savoring the time because you know soon there may be ice and snow.

Make your autumn evenings a time of rest—for you don't want to miss the season's beauty.

Lord, in autumn's kaleidoscope of colors, I see the wonders of You. Let me rest in Your creation.

Time Doesn't Stop

As for God, his way is perfect: The LORD's word is flawless; he shields all who take refuge in him. . . . It is God who arms me with strength and keeps my way secure.

—2 Samuel 22:31, 33

Is it really October already? If you feel as if the weeks and months are flying by, you aren't alone. While some days may seem to pass slowly, in the grand scheme of life, it all goes by so fast. Time doesn't stop—not even for a second. And with every birthday you celebrate, the years seem to slip by more and more quickly.

Though time often seems to fly by, you can rest assured that it isn't flying out of God's control. Even if your week has been a blur, He has overseen every single second of it; He even knows how many strands of hair fell off of your head yesterday. He isn't surprised by anything, and His plans are still active in your life, even if you feel as if you haven't had time to catch a breath. No, time isn't stopping, but you can rest in God's control.

Lord, it gives me such peace to know that You always are, and always will be, in control.

A Gift of Rest

Thanks be to God for his indescribable gift!

—2 Corinthians 9:15

Sometimes you receive a call, an e-mail, or a text that says your plans have been cancelled. You have been gifted with an unexpected opening in your day, and your calendar looks just a little less hectic. What do you do?

If at all possible, resist the urge to fill that opening with the next thing on your list. Pause before you grab your phone or laptop, and ask yourself, *Do I need this unexpected time to rejuvenate and rest? Could it be a gift?*

When space opens up, many times we react like a corporation or business, quickly filling that empty space. Instead, try to approach your calendar with a more human, less production-oriented mind-set. Let that space stay open. Don't try to cross a few more things off your checklist, set up that meeting, or cram in one more volunteer opportunity; stop and clear your head. Center your thinking. When you receive a gift of unexpected time, open yourself to rest.

When my calendar opens up unexpectedly, Lord, point me toward rest instead of my to-do list.

Perfect Focus

Those who know your name trust in you, for you, LORD, have never forsaken those who seek you.

—Psalm 9:10

Does your future look blurry? Are you uncertain of the direction your life is taking—or even *should* take? We all deal with that at one time or another. But take comfort. God is an expert at bringing blurry futures into perfect focus. He may do it only one step at a time, one moment at a time. But you can trust His vision for your life.

In those times when your future seems blurry and uncertain, turn to God for direction. He promises that He'll never forsake those who seek Him. He will never leave you lost and wandering. Rest in the guidance He will give you, trusting Him day by day, moment by moment, step by step.

If you are a follower of Christ, the Lord is with you always. He won't let you down, and He'll never forget your needs. Rest in knowing that the Lord will bring perfect focus to your life when you seek Him.

When my future looks blurry, I trust that You're in control and guiding my life, Lord.

Hardworking, Not Overworking

Lift up your eyes and look to the heavens: Who created all these? He who brings out the starry host one by one and calls forth each of them by name. Because of his great power and mighty strength, not one of them is missing.

—Isaiah 40:26

Dear friend, are you exhausted from overworking? Does the word *work* make your shoulders tense and head throb? Do you dread Monday morning with surprising intensity? You may be overworked.

Working hard is a good thing. It is a biblical mandate; the Lord wants us to be good, hard workers. But He also wants us to rest. He inserted the Sabbath into our week so we would have a rhythm of work and rest—it's the way our bodies need to function.

If you feel overworked and beaten down, turn your eyes toward heaven. The Lord is near. He knows your desire for rest. He has shoulders broad enough to carry you and your worries, and He is able to take your burdens away. Talk to Him. Turn to Him. He is ready to listen and help. Rest in Him.

Father God, I am overworked, weary, and discouraged. Please give me the rest I need.

The Half-Empty Glass

I have learned the secret of being content in any and every situation, whether well fed or hungry, whether living in plenty or in want. I can do all this through him who gives me strength.

—Philippians 4:12–13

Which sort of person are you—a "glass half-empty" or a "glass half-full"? Your answer can make all the difference when it comes to cultivating a mind-set of contentment. As humans, we naturally bend toward a desire for more, and we think fulfillment will come if only we just had _____. Though we may *know* that more stuff doesn't equal happiness, it's often a tough truth for our hearts to understand.

When you're feeling discontented, are you looking only at what you don't have? Are you seeing the glass as half-empty? Why not deliberately choose to see your glass as half-full? Living a "half-empty life" is exhausting. It keeps you focused on the disappointments, and it robs you of contentment and rest.

Choose to shift your thinking. Look around at your life: God has blessed you richly, even in difficult times. Open your eyes to the fullness of your cup. Rest in the Lord's abundant provision—and rejoice as He fills your cup to overflowing.

Change my heart, O Lord, and renew a right spirit within me.

A Different Rest

The LORD gave them rest on every side.

—Joshua 21:44

Most people think of rest merely as sleep—it's what you do when you fall into bed and close your eyes. But resting is not just physical; it's also a state of being.

Think about the past week. Has it been characterized by rest? Maybe you slept eight hours every night, but work stress kept your heart racing and shoulders tense. Or perhaps you took a few days off work, but those days were filled with back-to-back commitments. That's not rest, friend.

Rest is more than sleep and more than simply not working. True rest is being content in the Lord. It's living your life trusting Him and surrendering control over your life to Him. Rest means allowing not only your body to physically rest, but also your soul to spiritually rest. Find rest today, even in the midst of busyness and cares. Pass your worries to the Lord—and find contentment for the deepest part of your soul.

Father God, teach me to rest in all ways—physically, mentally, and spiritually.

When You Are Weak

For the sake of Christ, then, I am content with weaknesses, insults, hardships, persecutions, and calamities. For when I am weak, then I am strong.

—2 Corinthians 12:10 ESV

No one likes to feel weak or vulnerable—especially in our culture that prides itself on self-sufficiency and independence. But consider this: God's power is made perfect in your weakness. God says it Himself in His Word. The apostle Paul actually boasted of his own weakness, because in his weakness, he rested in the strength of the Lord. Paul's own agenda and desires were set aside, and the Lord was then able to work mightily in his life.

What does living in weakness look like? It doesn't mean letting others walk all over you or being lazy; it means fully relying on the Lord's strength rather than your own. Any hardship that comes up is simply handed to the Lord, and in His strength, He handles it.

You are strong when you are weak because that's when God's power is working most mightily through you. Rest from your striving, and believe that the Lord can handle it.

Jesus, may I become less so that You become greater.

Opportunity to Rest

Guide me in your truth and teach me, for you are God my Savior, and my hope is in you all day long.

—Psalm 25:5

Pause for a moment. Feel your lungs fill as you breathe deeply. Roll your shoulders back and let them relax. Revel in the stillness. You may not have many moments like this in a day—moments to reflect in the silence and to sit without feeling guilty. *Relish them.*

Though these moments may be few and far between, they will happen throughout the day—while you're sitting in the school pickup line, waiting for your oil to be changed, or parking the car after a long day of work. Seize those fleeting moments, the ones so small that they could easily be missed, and let yourself rest for just a few seconds.

Breathe in and out. Thank God for His presence. Ask Him for His help. Look to Him for guidance. Allow your heart and your mind to center on Him. And take this opportunity to rest.

Father, help me find small pockets of time to rest throughout my day.

Joy in the Lord

*You have been my hope, Sovereign LORD, my confidence since
my youth.*

—Psalm 71:5

We look for joy and fulfillment in many places: a new
house, our career, a relationship, a child, or a hobby.
While these things can certainly bring us happiness, they
can't give us the deep, soul-stirring, everlasting joy and
contentment we crave. Do you find yourself wanting more?
Do you feel a yearning that you can't quite fill? That's your
desire for God.

You can have the nicest clothes, biggest salary, most
loving family, or largest social group, but without a deep
satisfaction in the Lord, you'll feel empty. You won't feel
joyful or at rest; you'll feel hollow. Does that resonate
with you?

Ask the Lord to fill you with the joy that can only come
from Him. Make spending time with Him a priority and
converse with Him throughout your day. We all have a
longing within us that can only be filled by God, and He's
waiting to fill it. He's waiting to give you joy—and rest.

Oh, Lord, fill this hole in my life with Your presence and Your joy.

Timing Matters

The LORD is my rock, my fortress and my deliverer; my God is my rock, in whom I take refuge, my shield and the horn of my salvation, my stronghold.

—Psalm 18:2

God doesn't always answer our prayers according to our timeline. Yes, sometimes prayers are answered instantaneously, but often the answer takes far longer than we'd like. And sometimes, the answers just aren't what we'd expected or hoped.

God's timing matters. His reasons for when and how He answers our prayers may be beyond our ability to see at the moment, but that's because He sees the bigger picture. We can only live in this present moment, but God is omnipresent, living eternally in each and every moment. He sees how all the many pieces fit together, and He is working all these things together for your good.

Find rest in God's timing. Know that it may not be what you want, and you may have to lay down your own desires, but God is working for your eternal good. He is trustworthy. Rest in the belief that His perfect answer is coming, in His perfect time.

Father, help me trust that You answer my prayers perfectly and at the perfect time.

Great Is His Faithfulness

Who is like you, Lord God Almighty? You, Lord, are mighty, and your faithfulness surrounds you.

—Psalm 89:8

As the nights become cooler and the leaves change, it's clear that autumn is upon us. And with autumn comes a time of reflection. It is a good time to think of all you can be grateful for—even if it's been a difficult year.

Some years are filled with joy and happiness and blessings, while others are filled with grief and loss, anger and confusion. But whether it's been a wonderful year or a challenging, heart-wrenching year, one thing is true: God is faithful.

The song "Great Is Thy Faithfulness" speaks to that truth: "Great is Thy faithfulness, O God my Father; there is no shadow of turning with Thee; Thou changest not, Thy compassions they fail not; as Thou hast been, Thou forever wilt be." God doesn't change; His compassion for you does not waver; He remains the same forever and ever. What a merciful God. What a gracious Father. Rest in the certainty of His faithfulness.

Lord, may I always sing of Your faithfulness even when I'm in a difficult season.

Eyes Wide Open

Sing to him, sing praise to him; tell of all his wonderful acts.
—1 Chronicles 16:9

If you've ever taken a walk with a young child, you know it's often more stopping than walking. She'll want to look at every bug, crack in the sidewalk, fallen leaf, and budding flower. He'll bend down to inspect a colony of ants and look up to see the airplane roaring overhead. Children live with their eyes wide open.

But as we grow into adults, something changes. Pebbles and grass are exchanged for phones and laptop screens. That sense of wonder is replaced with worry and stress. Instead of taking our time, we rush, rush, rush. We don't stop to see the beauty around us.

Slow down and keep your eyes wide open. Notice the way your spouse laughs or your dog settles in the sunlight. Breathe in the aroma of fresh bread as you pass the bakery. Savor your cup of coffee. Living with eyes wide open will invite more wonder into your life—and a more restful, childlike spirit.

Jesus, help me recapture my wonder for Your earth and my life.

H-E-L-P

The wisdom that comes from heaven is first of all pure; then peace-loving, considerate, submissive, full of mercy and good fruit, impartial and sincere.

—James 3:17

elp. It's a short word, but for many, it's so difficult to say. But asking for help isn't about helplessness; asking for help is about **H**onesty, **E**nlisting others, the **L**ove of God, and **P**rayer.

Honesty means acknowledging that you are human, and you can't do it all. You don't have infinite time, energy, brain space, or resources. So at times you need to *enlist others*, which means actively reaching out for help. It isn't shameful; it's a step toward living a more restful life. And it allows others the freedom to admit that they too need help.

You can also enlist God's help, trusting that He will provide it. Why? Because of His enormous *love for you*. And how can you seek God's assistance? Through *prayer*. Open your mouth and heart, and spill out all your worries and struggles before the Lord.

Seek Him, seek H-E-L-P, and find rest.

Lord, give me the humility, honesty, and courage to reach out for help.

He Wants to Give You Rest

*"Are you tired? Worn out? . . . Come to me. Get away with me
and you'll recover your life. I'll show you how to take a real rest."*

—Matthew 11:28 THE MESSAGE

When Jesus called for the tired and worn out to come to Him, He wasn't offering empty words. He didn't say it to be nice or to gain more followers; Jesus said He would give rest because that's what He wanted to do—and the Lord always honors His Word.

If you worry that asking God for rest is burdensome or bothersome to Him, take heart, because just the opposite is true. He is waiting for you to come to Him; He *wants* you to ask Him for rest. He longs for all those who are weary to have rest and to have it to the fullest.

What a breath of encouragement! Jesus declared that He would show us *how* to rest. That is a promise. That is a declaration. He will give you rest—real rest—dear friend. Come away with Him.

Lord Jesus, I come to You now. Please show me how to really rest.

Trust His Leading

Do you not know? Have you not heard? The Lord is the everlasting God, the Creator of the ends of the earth. He will not grow tired or weary, and his understanding no one can fathom.

—Isaiah 40:28

Walking with your eyes closed is scary, especially in unfamiliar territory. You don't know where the bumps and obstacles are, and you're not sure if the path will take a turn in the next step or the next mile. Your steps are tentative, full of fear and uncertainty.

Life can often feel that way because the future is uncertain. You don't know when the stormy season will pass or when your time of peace will end. But remember this: the ultimate Guide is right beside you. He knows the trail, He knows exactly how many steps until the next turn, and He knows exactly how to get out of the wilderness. With His guidance, you can walk forward with confidence.

Have you been looking to the ultimate Guide for His leading? If so, you know the remarkable rest that comes with following His lead. Trust His steps, and don't veer off His path; He knows the way.

You are my Guide, Comforter, and Companion, Jesus. May I always follow Your lead.

The Present Day

Everyone was amazed and gave praise to God. They were filled with awe and said, "We have seen remarkable things today."

—Luke 5:26

How often do you think about the next hour, day, month, or year? How often have you thought, *I can't wait until . . . ?* Do you find yourself wishing today would hurry up and be over so that you can get on with your real life? It's understandable, but try to remember: this present day is God's gift to you. Open it up; enjoy it fully.

In this present moment, God gives you breath. He keeps your heart beating. He woke you up this morning, and He reveals Himself to you all throughout the day—through the kindness of a stranger, the colorful autumn leaves, the rich orange hue of pumpkins at the market. Don't be so focused on the future that you miss the present; it is filled with God's blessings and gifts. There is much to be enjoyed in this day. Look for it, and then rest in the joy of this present moment.

Jesus, when I'm wishing time would pass by, remind me that today is a gift from You.

Don't Turn Away

"A Samaritan, as he traveled, came where the man was; and when he saw him, he took pity on him."

—Luke 10:33

A Jewish man was traveling from Jerusalem to Jericho when he was attacked by robbers, beaten, and left for dead. A priest and a Levite both passed him by, but it was a Samaritan—despised by the Jews—who stopped to help.

Most Christians know this story of the good Samaritan by heart. But how often do we stop instead of passing by? We get so busy in our own lives that it's easy to turn a blind eye to someone's need. Yet, in ignoring someone in need, whether a lonely individual at church or an ill neighbour, we become just like that uncaring priest and Levite. And, though ignoring another's need may bring rest to our physical life, it will not bring rest to our souls.

The next time you see someone in need, stop to offer love and compassion instead of hurrying by. Yes, you may find yourself weary in body, but you'll be blessed with a rested soul.

Father God, help me walk toward those in need, even if it's not convenient.

The Big Picture

"Consider how the wild flowers grow. They do not labor or spin. Yet I tell you, not even Solomon in all his splendor was dressed like one of these."

—Luke 12:27

Have you ever helped with a big event? Maybe you planned the whole thing, or you were one of many tasked with helping execute the plan. Big events require so many details and decisions. It can be easy to get caught up in the most minute aspects and lose sight of the reason behind it all—the charity behind the golf tournament, the person honored by the party, the couple in love versus the show of the wedding.

The same thing can happen in life. There are so many details, both big and small, that can consume our lives— paying the bills, planning for retirement, vacations, kids and college, appointments, and relationships. All the details of life can certainly seem overwhelming, but in the grand scheme of things, life is about glorifying God and living for Him.

Instead of stressing over all the details of life, why not simply look at the big picture: God. Find rest in trusting Him with the details.

Lord God, remind me that life is less about all the details and more about You.

Resting in the Word

He will not let your foot slip—he who watches over you will not slumber; indeed, he who watches over Israel will neither slumber nor sleep.

—Psalm 121:3–4

Hebrews 4:12 calls the Word of God "alive and active." When you read the Bible, do you believe that? Or do you find yourself thinking of it as simply a collection of stories and songs written thousands of years ago?

Dear friend, God's Word is His own voice and wisdom speaking to us as we walk through this journey of life. It gives wisdom, it teaches life-changing lessons, and it speaks God's truth. Do you believe the Bible when it says we are more than conquerors (Romans 8:37)? Do you rejoice knowing that God never slumbers because He's watching over you (Psalm 121:4)?

And at the end of the Bible, in Revelation, God reveals how our story will end. He will conquer all, this world will be redeemed, and we will be with Him for eternity. Rest in the true and living words of the Bible, and rest in its promises. God will keep every one of them.

Thank You for Your Word, Father. I am grateful for its teachings and for Your promises.

Patience in Prayer

How long, LORD, how long? Turn, LORD, and deliver me; save me because of your unfailing love.

—Psalm 6:3–4

Prayers are . . . mysterious. They flow upward in tears, in words, and in songs. They aren't always fully formed or thought out. And sometimes, the only word we seem to be able to pray is *help*.

Whatever your prayer, if you are coming to the Lord with your whole heart, you can be full of expectation. He is a living God who does mighty and awesome works for His children, and He loves to answer prayer—in small ways, in large ways, in ways that exceed your expectations and even your imagination. Answered prayers aren't luck or merely happy coincidences—they are the God of the universe orchestrating the tiniest details of your life into beautiful blessings.

If you're waiting for a prayer to be answered, keep pounding on the door of heaven. And rest in knowing that your prayer will be answered—in the fullness of time, in the wisdom of God, and with His unfailing love.

Father, I give You my prayers, and I wait to see Your power working in great and mighty ways.

Comfort in a Broken World

May these words of my mouth and this meditation of my heart be
pleasing in your sight, LORD, my Rock and my Redeemer.

—Psalm 19:14

Jesus predicted that in this world we would have trouble, and the truth of that can be overwhelming at times. Our world is full of greed, ugly politics, starving families, impoverished countries, and life-threatening crime. The news headlines are often shocking and disturbing. Sometimes it seems that the world can't get any worse—but then it does.

When the world's brokenness is too much to bear, turn your eyes to Jesus. Perhaps that sounds like a cliché, but He is the only way to find comfort and peace in this broken world.

Jesus walked this earth. He understands the burden you feel, because He experienced it too. But He overcame this world, and He rose up from the grave to give you eternal life. He conquered sin and death; evil doesn't get the final word. Jesus came so that we could have hope. Turn to Him, and let Him turn your sorrows into gladness, your weariness into rest.

Jesus, my heart is troubled by this world's brokenness, but I thank
You for making me whole.

Approach the Throne

Let us then approach God's throne of grace with confidence, so that we may receive mercy and find grace to help us in our time of need.

—Hebrews 4:16

Have you ever avoided prayer? If so, you're one of many Christians who have resisted coming to the throne of God. Perhaps you're embarrassed or fearful, frustrated or filled with shame. Yet, no matter your sorrow or sin, as a child of God, you can freely and boldly approach the Lord without fear of condemnation.

Hebrews 4:16 welcomes us to approach the throne of God's grace with confidence. Instead of receiving any sort of berating or anger, we'll receive mercy and grace. Instead of being looked upon with wrath and judgment, we'll be viewed through the lens of God's love, compassion, and forgiveness.

Go before the Lord with joy and with confidence, for He longs to hear your prayers, to free you from all your burdens, and to fill you with heavenly love and peace and rest.

Lord, teach me to approach Your throne with confidence and expectation.

The Gift of Silence

It is good to wait quietly for the salvation of the LORD.

—Lamentations 3:26

Our world is loud. It's busy. It's fast. Silence is a stranger that, so often, we run away from. We put in our headphones, turn on the television, flip through the radio stations. When is the last time you simply let your world go silent?

When we rush through our days and weeks in a roar of constant noise, God's still, small voice tends to get muddled. We stop listening for Him and instead listen to the loudest voices and the most urgent and pressing priorities. We can't hear God's voice when we're filling our ears with everything else.

Dear friend, embrace the silence. Sit in quiet stillness with the Lord today. It might feel uncomfortable, and you may even feel jittery. You'll probably feel the urge to fidget or scroll through your phone or check the news. But it's in the quiet that God's still, small voice is best heard. Silence the noise and find rest in listening to Him.

Here I am, Lord. I'm stepping away from the noise and listening for Your voice.

Smoothing Out a Rough Start

*So now faith, hope, and love abide, these three; but the greatest of
these is love.*

—1 Corinthians 13:13 ESV

The coffeepot broke. Your child woke up with a cold—or
you did. You've yelled at your spouse, and it's not even
6 a.m. yet. You forgot to pack your lunch, and now you're
late for work. When the morning begins badly, it's hard
not to let it affect the rest of your day. But there is good
news: even on the roughest of days, the Lord can smooth
out a bumpy start.

Try praying on the commute. Forgot lunch? Treat
yourself to lunch out with a friend or a good book, or a
sandwich in the sunshine. Yelled at your spouse? Apologize
with a flower, goofy text, or favorite meal. Rely on God's
faithfulness and His power to turn all things to good.

He is One who turned water into wine, death into
resurrection, ashes into beauty, and nothingness into creation. He makes all things new. When your day seems like
it's turning into a disaster, call on the Lord; He is faithful
to respond.

*Father, some days start out so rough, but I know You're faithful in
all my days.*

By Quiet Waters

Like cold water to a thirsty soul, so is good news from a far country.
—Proverbs 25:25 ESV

There's something about water that's so calming. Whether you're sitting on the sand by the ocean, wading through a cold stream, watching the sunset over the lake, or hiking near a waterfall, water settles and soothes the soul. That's why so many people love falling asleep to the sound of the ocean's waves, raindrops drumming against the roof, or a babbling brook. When David declares that the Lord is his shepherd in Psalm 23, he says, "He leads me beside quiet waters, he refreshes my soul." To be led by quiet waters, to be refreshed and rejuvenated—that is what the Lord offers to you.

Even if you don't live near water, you can still find that quiet refreshment for your soul. Ask the Lord to lead you beside still waters today. He desires to give you rest, even in the midst of your busy and hectic life. Relax by the still, quiet waters of God's goodness and grace today.

Lord, You are my Shepherd. Lead me beside quiet waters and refresh my soul.

It Is Better to Give

Let each one give [thoughtfully and with purpose] just as he has decided in his heart, not grudgingly or under compulsion, for God loves a cheerful giver [and delights in the one whose heart is in his gift].

—2 Corinthians 9:7 AMP

You've heard it said, "It is better to give than receive." But do you believe it? Do you live it? And why—in this world that tells us that *getting* is more important—should you give? Because our Savior did. Jesus came into this world and gave . . . *all*. He laid down His life for us to give us an example of how to live.

Since we are all so richly blessed, how about focusing on finding rest in the joy of giving to someone today? Even if you feel you have little to give, you have something. Give a smile, give a meal, give whatever you can. Through blessing others, you are acting as the hands and feet of Jesus. You may not receive a thank you, and you may not even receive an acknowledgement, but you will receive joy. And with it, you'll find contentment and true rest for your soul.

Father, open my eyes to all the ways I can bless others with what You've given me.

Faith over Fear

Trust in the LORD forever, for the LORD, the LORD himself, is the Rock eternal.

—Isaiah 26:4

Fear is invisible, but extremely powerful. Like a spider's web, it clings to everything it touches. It can be paralyzing, overwhelming, all-encompassing, and life-altering. Fear runs rampant in our world.

But as God's beloved children, we do not need to give way to fear. It doesn't have to be a part of our lives. Instead, we can rest in peaceful confidence, knowing that the almighty God of the universe takes care of us. He holds us in the palm of His hand—the same hand that filled the oceans and flung the stars into the farthest reaches of the heavens. He, the One who never grows weary, watches over us while we sleep and commands the sun to rise up to greet us each morning. The Lord our God is greater than all our fears.

Let go of your fears today. Lay them at the feet of God. Breathe in His promises of provision and exhale any doubt. The Lord is faithful to protect His children. Rest in His faithfulness to you.

I give my fears to You, Lord Jesus. Thank You for Your promised relief and peace.

The Lord Goes Before You

It is the LORD who goes before you. He will be with you; he will not leave you or forsake you. Do not fear or be dismayed.

—Deuteronomy 31:8 ESV

When you look ahead into the future days and weeks, you may feel overwhelmed. There are appointments, obligations, social events, and so many demands on your time. Your heart pounds as you wonder, *How will I get through this day, let alone the next week?*

When Moses was speaking to the fearful Israelites, he said in Deuteronomy 31:6, "Be strong and courageous. Do not fear or be in dread of them, for it is the LORD your God who goes with you. He will not leave you or forsake you" (ESV). Dear friend, those words are also for you.

And not only does the Lord promise to be with you, He also promises to go before you. He knows what you will be up against in the next hour, in the next week, in the next decade. And He goes before you to prepare the way—what a comfort!

Today, trust God to give you the wisdom and resources to meet this day's challenges. Rest in His promised provision.

Lord, thank You for going before me; I will trust in You today.

Relationships Matter

"Love one another. As I have loved you, so you must love one another."

—John 13:34

When was the last time you really enjoyed your family? Really looked at your spouse and asked how he or she was doing? Can you recall the last time you went out to dinner with your parents and basked in their company instead of rushing off to your next commitment? Are you nurturing those relationships with your closest friends, or are you choosing to work late nights and weekends at the office instead?

Life is short, and with each passing year, the time seems to fly by even more quickly. Making time for family and close friends is so important, but with packed schedules and obligations vying for our attention, it often gets pushed to the side.

Be intentional today. Family matters. Friends matter. Push *pause* on your day, afternoon, or evening, and really invest in a family member or friend. And then rest in the joy of your time together.

I get so caught up in everyday life, Father. Help me make my loved ones a priority.

The Words of My Mouth

May these words of my mouth and this meditation of my heart be pleasing in your sight, LORD, my Rock and my Redeemer.

—Psalm 19:14

Your words have power. Not only the power to impact someone else, but also the power to alter your own thinking. Ponder this: if your words are always full of complaints about life's busyness and difficulties, you're going to begin believing that life is negative.

Why not try a different way? Instead of distress, speak words of hope in the Lord and joy in His faithfulness. When you remind yourself of these truths, you'll begin believing them and acting on them—and filling your life with positivity and praise.

When negative words begin springing to your lips, try giving thanks to the Lord instead. When despair creeps into your conversation, declare the truths of who God is and what He says in His Word. Your Lord brings light, not darkness; He brings peace, not strife; and He offers hope, not despair. Rest in the power of praising Him.

May the words of my mouth always be pleasing to You, Lord.

NOVEMBER

*There remains, then, a Sabbath-rest for
the people of God; for anyone who enters
God's rest also rests from their works, just
as God did from his.*

—Hebrews 4:9–10

The Potter's Work

O Lord, you are our Father; we are the clay, and you are our potter; we are all the work of your hand.

—Isaiah 64:8 ESV

When a potter begins her work, she has a slab of clay. It's not particularly memorable, and it's certainly not beautiful. But with skill and patience, she carefully shapes the clay, according to her own special design, transforming it into something useful and beautiful.

We are all like that lump of clay, works in progress in the hands of the Master Potter. And we are being transformed, according to His own design, into something useful and beautiful. He is shaping our hearts, minds, and souls to be more like Him, patiently crafting our lives into a masterpiece. A masterpiece that will bring glory to Him.

Let the Master Potter mold you and shape you. Trust Him to smooth out the lumps and straighten out the uneven areas, to make you useful and beautiful. Rest in His hands.

Thank You, Father God, for loving me as I am, while working to make me more like You.

Your Team

Let us therefore make every effort to do what leads to peace and to mutual edification.

—Romans 14:19

Watching the Olympics can be an emotional experience. Athletes go through years and years of training, and, depending on the event, it all culminates in just a few short moments. Sometimes, athletes have only seconds to prove they're the best in the world. Now that's pressure!

When athletes talk about their training and the efforts that led them to the Olympics, they mention their drive, desire, and love for the sport. But they also mention everyone who helped them reach that point: their team. Parents, coaches, personal trainers, nutritionists, and teammates are all incredibly important to an Olympian's career. They provide encouragement when the days are tough, strategy when success seems impossible, and massive amounts of support.

Who is your team? Do you have friends and family cheering you on and supporting you? Life is a team effort. Lean on your team when you need to rest.

Father, thank You for my team. Give me the courage to lean on them.

Listen to Your Body

Praise the LORD, my soul, and forget not all his benefits—who forgives all your sins and heals all your diseases, who redeems your life from the pit and crowns you with love and compassion.

—Psalm 103:2–4

It's usually easy to tell when your body is getting sick. You begin to feel aches and pains, and you might even begin to feel feverish. Perhaps you wake up with a sore throat, or you simply can't go another minute without a nap. When sickness is coming, your body gives you warning signs.

In the same way, when exhaustion is coming, your body will let you know. You may feel constantly fatigued, depressed, or discouraged. You may want to throw your alarm clock across the room when it wakes you in the morning. Listen to your body; it's time to start slowing down and allow yourself to rest.

Let yourself sleep for an extra hour. Ask for help on that overwhelming work project. Tell your spouse you need more help around the house or with the kids. Say no to more obligations. If your body is telling you to rest, listen—and then rest.

Lord, my body feels so weary. Bless me with rest today.

Living in Gratitude

Sing and make music from your heart to the Lord, always giving thanks to God the Father for everything, in the name of our Lord Jesus Christ.

—Ephesians 5:19–20

During the days leading up to Thanksgiving, it's common to list all the things you're grateful for. But gratitude isn't just for the holidays; it's for every day. What if each and every day, you sought out things to be grateful for?

This week, open your eyes to God's gifts in your life. With each new morning, thank Him for yesterday's grace. And every evening, thank Him for tomorrow's new mercies. God fills our lives with so many good gifts—the laughter of children, hot turkey on a cold afternoon, and red cardinals against white snow. His gifts are all around; you only need eyes to see and a heart turned toward thanksgiving.

Cultivating gratitude is an essential part of finding true contentment and rest. How would your life be different if you were to live in gratitude each day, all year long?

Father, open my eyes to see Your gifts, and open my heart to praise You.

The Peacemakers

Peacemakers who sow in peace reap a harvest of righteousness.

—James 3:18

Conflict is inevitable in our broken world. Because Christians are sinners, not every one of our interactions with others is going to be perfect. We will be hurt and we will hurt others—even those we love. It's a hard truth, but there is good news: God uses us as His peacemakers. Romans 12:18 says, "If possible, so far as it depends on you, live peaceably with all" (ESV). While you can't control what others do, you can control yourself.

As far as it depends on you, run toward peace. Choose calm instead of anger, and bring reconciliation to others through your actions and words. If you need to confront others, do so in love and humility. Being a peacemaker isn't passive, weak, or meek; it requires a quiet strength that trusts completely in the Lord and in His way. And it is utterly needed in our world today.

By embodying the spirit of a peacemaker, you will impact those around you. You will point them toward the God of peace. And you will all be closer to rest.

Lord, help me rely on Your strength and be a peacemaker in every situation.

Sweet Like Honey

Gracious words are like a honeycomb, sweetness to the soul and health to the body.

—Proverbs 16:24 ESV

Did you know there are more than three hundred different types of honey in the US alone? The flavor and color of honey depends on the blossoms the honeybees visit. Some bees feast on alfalfa, which produces a very light honey, while others eat from avocado blossoms, resulting in a darker, buttery-tasting honey. Whatever the bees feed on is reflected in the resulting honey.

What about you? Do the words of your mouth and your actions throughout the day reflect someone who's been "feeding" on the Word of the Lord? Just like honeybees, our lives and the fruit we bear will reflect what we've been feeding on.

When you feast upon the Word, your own words become sweet and gracious, your thoughts become noble and upright, and your heart is transformed. The Lord desires your life to pour forth like the sweetest honey, and in giving others a taste, you will help them find rest and hope in Him.

May I feast on Your words and Your truths, Lord, so that my words will be sweet like honey!

Weekend of Rest

The promise of "arrival" and "rest" is still there for God's people. God himself is at rest. And at the end of the journey we'll surely rest with God.

—Hebrews 4:9–10 THE MESSAGE

When you're headed into the weekend, it's full of possibilities. You have *two full days* to get things done, to relax, and to enjoy time away from the Monday-through-Friday routine. But unlike the rest of the week, the weekend usually goes by much too fast and you're left wishing you had one more day.

Yes, the weekend *is* a great time to catch up on chores and errands, but are you trying to do too much? Going into this weekend, make an effort to set aside time to intentionally rest. Take a nap; take a walk. Listen to a sermon, a concert, or the crickets while you count the stars. Rock in a porch swing, sit and watch the sunset, or sip coffee with the sunrise. Do something to feed your soul.

This weekend, instead of being bullied by your to-do list, let rest be your first priority.

Father, may my priority this weekend be to rest, and may I rest to the fullest.

Nighttime Rest

By day the LORD commands his steadfast love, and at night his song is with me, a prayer to the God of my life.

—Psalm 42:8 ESV

*T*icktock, ticktock. As the clock's hands wind down at the end of the day, they signal us to slow down and rest. The sun has set, birds are in their nests, and the roads are cleared of rush-hour traffic. It's evening, and stillness is overtaking the busyness of the day.

While your clock's hands are winding down, allow yourself to wind down as well. Spend a few moments on the couch with your loved ones. Take time to visit with the Lord. Enjoy the twilight, count the stars, dim the lights, read a book. Your heart rate will slow, your breathing will become deeper and more steady, and your muscles will slowly relax.

Winding down is a gift. It's an invitation to give your body and mind the rest that they need. As the hour gets later, may your own routine wind down and settle into an evening of quiet rest.

Teach me, Lord, to rest in the nighttime so that I can feel relaxed and ready for tomorrow.

The Ultimate Satisfaction

God is able to bless you abundantly, so that in all things at all times,
having all that you need, you will abound in every good work.

—2 Corinthians 9:8

God will meet all your needs. Yes, all of them. In fact, only He can fulfill your truest and deepest needs for purpose, contentment, peace, and salvation. If dissatisfaction is stealing your rest today, you're not alone. While we live on this earth, we will deal with longing for something that seems unreachable. It's a symptom of being human. God placed a longing within us that only He can fill.

Some people turn to the stuff of this world, to others, or to jobs or hobbies for fulfillment. And while those things may temporarily bring happiness or distraction, only God can provide eternal fulfillment. He can satisfy you when nothing and no one else does. That doesn't mean you should give up all your hopes and dreams for happiness on this earth. It simply means that God has more for you, better for you, divinely perfect for you. You can rely on Him to work beyond your understanding. That's a truth you can rest in.

Lord, I know that only You can truly satisfy; fill me with Your presence.

The Lord Is Near

"I tell you, whatever you ask for in prayer, believe that you have received it, and it will be yours."

—Mark 11:24

If you read through the book of Psalms, you'll know that David endured times of great pain in his life. Many times, he cried out to God in despair, wept with sorrow, and begged God to come to his aid and defeat his enemies.

Maybe you're feeling a whole lot of pain right now. Your heart is broken, and the circumstances you're in feel bleak. Perhaps it's physical pain you're battling, or even the loss of a loved one. Do you feel lonely? Do you feel sad? Turn your eyes to heaven; the Lord *is* near.

Do as David did; call upon the Lord continually. Open up your heart to Him. God doesn't need wordy, poetic prayers; simple and open honesty is all He seeks. And you don't have to have everything figured out—that's what God is there for. Just call out to Him in your pain, believe in Him, trust Him, and He will give you rest.

Oh, Lord my God, I cry out to You. Rescue me and give me rest.

"Indulge" in Rest

After bidding them farewell, He left for the mountain to pray.

—Mark 6:46 NASB

What would happen if you took the day off? If you simply put life—with all its obligations, work, errands, and responsibilities—on hold. Would the world end? No, of course not. So why not indulge in a little rest?

You might not be able to take a whole day off, but what if you took off for just a couple of hours? If you're really swamped, at least take a break for lunch—a real break, not the eat-at-your-desk or the eat-in-the-car-on-the-way-back-from-the-drive-through kind of lunch. Sneak away for a twenty-minute power nap. Indulge in a little room to breathe, to goof off, to daydream, to be completely unproductive.

And by the way, this taking a break thing isn't really an indulgence—though it may feel as if it is at times. It's something you *need* to refresh your body, mind, and soul. So go ahead. Take a day off. "Indulge" in a little rest.

Thank You for this day, Father. I think I'll enjoy it by "indulging" in a little rest.

The Afternoon Slump

"I am the LORD your God who takes hold of your right hand and says to you, Do not fear; I will help you."

—Isaiah 41:13

Do you ever hit an afternoon slump? You just ate lunch, you're feeling a little groggy, and even a double-shot of espresso can't get you going. You may not have time for a two-hour nap, but what about turning to something other than caffeine to combat your low energy?

Open the windows and breathe in the fresh air. Walk around outside for a few minutes. Munch on some fruit. Turn on some music and dance. Do some jumping jacks. Be silly with your kids, your friends, or even your pet. Stretch and pray. You'll be surprised what just a little shake-up can do.

When the afternoon slump creeps up again, don't just chow down on empty sugar and caffeine; instead, fight it with activity, a healthy snack, laughter, or prayer. Not only will you be more clear-headed and focused; you'll simply find a more restful way to live.

When I hit the afternoon slump, remind me of ways I can be energized instead of discouraged, Lord.

Modeling Rest

These commandments that I give you today are to be on your hearts. Impress them on your children. Talk about them when you sit at home and when you walk along the road, when you lie down and when you get up.

—Deuteronomy 6:6–7

When a baby first begins trying to speak, he'll mimic the sounds you make. If you repeatedly say *mama* or *dada*, he'll soon pick up those sounds and begin saying them himself. And eventually, he'll begin repeating other sounds and words as well. Parents soon learn to be careful about what little ones hear, because they're bound to repeat it!

The same principle applies to living a life of rest. Somewhere, there's a little someone watching you—whether it's your own children, nieces and nephews, grandchildren, or the children at church. If you're living a fast-paced life, never taking time to rest or be alone with God, they notice.

Live the way you want these little ones to live. Model a life that balances responsibilities and rest. Take time out to be silly; spend time with family and friends; worship the Lord. Model love and joy—and rest.

Lord, help me be a good example for these little ones You've placed in my life.

Know My Heart

Search me, God, and know my heart; test me and know my anxious thoughts. See if there is any offensive way in me, and lead me in the way everlasting.

—Psalm 139:23–24

Have you ever confessed one of your deepest, darkest secrets . . . and then waited with trepidation for a response? Hopefully, that response was filled with love and grace—for we've *all* fallen short of God's perfection. But if it wasn't, hear this truth: God already knows all your deepest, darkest sins, and He still loves you.

In Psalm 139, the psalmist asks God to search his heart, to know his thoughts, and to lead him. Why? Because he knows that God is a caring God who desires to make him more like Christ. While some believers may simply want God to look at their outward acts of service and compassion, the psalmist asks God to look within.

When you ask God to examine you, He'll show you how to be more pleasing to Him. He'll lead you on the right path, and He'll transform your life inside and out. He will wash you spotlessly clean of every sin. Rest in the safety and certainty of knowing that you are His own beloved child.

Lord, test me, examine me, and know my anxious thoughts. Lead me in the way everlasting.

Cultivating a Habit of Rest

Put off your old self, which is being corrupted by its deceitful desires . . . put on the new self, created to be like God in true righteousness and holiness.

—Ephesians 4:22–24

Just like making your bed or exercising regularly, creating a new habit—such as making time to rest—takes practice and commitment. First, you must *decide* that you both need and want rest. Next, you must plan *how* you will rest. Then, take that first step toward completing your plan, and try your very hardest to stick to it. Sure, you may mess up along the way, but just get back up and try again and again and again until the habit of rest is formed.

If you want rest to be a regular component of your life, you'll need to make it a habit. Life is busy, and it's easy to forgo rest. But if you've made it a habit, you'll more automatically incorporate it into your life. Whether it's a morning quiet time, journaling, prayer, or simply committing to sleeping enough at night, rest is a habit that will bless you for the remainder of your life.

Lord, please give me the discipline to make rest a habit in my life.

Breathing in God's Peace

"Blessed are the peacemakers, for they will be called children of God."

—Matthew 5:9

Have you ever noticed a physical reaction when you're worried? For many, a pounding heart, sweating, shaking, shortness of breath, difficulty swallowing, nausea, and dizziness begin to take hold of the body. It may not be obvious at first, but as your worries increase, the physical symptoms become stronger.

Have you felt any of those symptoms this week? Do you feel surprised by how well those words describe you? Beloved, this life has many worries, but our God is bigger and stronger than them all.

Take a deep breath. As you breathe in, remind yourself of God's promises and faithfulness. As you breathe out, imagine all your worries flowing out of your body—because where the Spirit of the Lord is, there is freedom and no place for worry. Continue this deep breathing until your body relaxes and the Lord calms you. God is bigger than any trouble or worry; ask Him to fill you with His Spirit of peace.

I'm full of worry, but I know You're able to take this from me. Come quickly, Lord.

Every Day Has Goodness

Let us hold unswervingly to the hope we profess, for he who promised is faithful.

—Hebrews 10:23

At the end of the day, do you ever feel defeated by everything you weren't able to accomplish? Even the best-laid plans can fail because life is often unpredictable and messy. If you weren't able to finish everything you needed or wanted to get done, today can still be a good day; you do not need to feel defeated.

Think about all that you *were* able to do and to experience today, from the smallest to the largest thing. Maybe you made the bed and put bread in the toaster. You got children clothed and to the bus on time. You made a casserole or mowed the lawn for someone who's sick. You encouraged a colleague. You laughed with your mom. You reassured a friend. Every day has good in it because Christ is in every day.

Don't allow disappointments to rule your thoughts. Celebrate the good you experience, and thank God for blessing you with another day.

Thank You for being with me, Lord, through the highs and lows of each day.

Jesus First

There is a friend who sticks closer than a brother.

—Proverbs 18:24

You can find rest in naps, nature, and silence. You can be rejuvenated with time away and time to think. But true rest and true rejuvenation come only through Jesus; He alone is our ultimate resting place.

How is your relationship with Jesus today? Have you been spending time with Him, or has the daily grind of life kept you away? Have you been bringing your troubles to the cross, or have you been bearing your own burdens? Perhaps it's time to seek rest in Him today.

Dear friend, put your relationship with Jesus first. He is your best Friend and greatest Comforter. He is the wisest Counselor and Most High King. He knows every pain, every worry—and He is able to take each one from you. Jesus is waiting to spend time with you. Come to Him now; the chores, social media, and your inbox can all wait. Sit with Jesus first; rest in the presence of your Savior.

Too often I put other things ahead of You, Lord. Help me to seek You first.

The Homiest Home

My people will live in safety, quietly at home. They will be at rest.
—Isaiah 32:18 NLT

When you picture a homey sort of home, what comes to mind? A crackling fireplace, a warm meal, lots of laughter, and a comfortable bed? Perhaps you picture your grandmother's home with all its quirks and charm. The very best homes are those places where you feel comfortable and relaxed. They're not usually model homes, and you won't find them on the cover of a magazine, but they're homey—and that makes all the difference.

Does your home inspire such feelings? If not, perhaps it's time to make some changes. That doesn't mean you need a complete redesign or all new furniture and rugs. Instead, hominess begins with a restful atmosphere of love. Your home should be a safe escape from the world, where all are made to feel welcome and wanted. The homiest homes are outfitted with frequent hugs, bright smiles, and warm encouragement.

Whether yours is a home for one or for twenty-one, make it a haven of restful welcome for all who enter it.

God, I pray that Your love so fills me that it spills out into my home.

Taste and See

Taste and see that the LORD is good; blessed is the one who takes refuge in him.

—Psalm 34:8

Many major product brands use blind taste tests to compare their brand to another brand. In 1975, Pepsi began doing a blind taste test to try to show their soda's superiority to Coca-Cola. They had shoppers taste both sodas without knowing which brand was in each cup. Then the taster indicated which brand he or she preferred. Since then, other companies have followed suit and performed blind taste tests to see how their product compares to others.

Blind taste tests are really helpful in product research, but there is one test that is not needed—for the Lord will win every single time. He will not disappoint tasters in any way. He will always be the top-rated because He is perfect. Nothing compares to Him.

Psalm 34 asks readers to "taste and see that the LORD is good"—because the psalmist knows nothing will satisfy like the Lord. Nothing comes close. Rest, today, in the delightful goodness of the Lord; savor and be satisfied.

Father, please remind me of Your goodness today.

Bitter into Sweet

He cried to the LORD, and the LORD showed him a log, and he threw it into the water, and the water became sweet.

—Exodus 15:25 ESV

Do you remember the story of Moses and the bitter waters of Marah? Soon after the miracle at the Red Sea, Moses and the Israelites were searching for water in the wilderness. But when they finally found it, in a place called Marah, they could not drink it because the water was bitter.

So the people grumbled; even though they'd just witnessed a number of miracles, they complained. And instead of refusing to give His griping people sweet, clean water, the Lord told Moses to throw a log into the water. Moses did, and the bitter water became sweet. Only God has the power to turn something bitter into something sweet.

If you're going through a bitter time, collapse into the arms of the Father—for He can turn the bitter into sweet. The transformation may not be instant, and it may not come in ways you expect, but He will take care of you and provide for you. Find rest in anticipating the sweetness.

Lord, even in bitter times, let me not be blinded to Your sweetness.

More Than Enough

No eye has seen, no ear has heard, and no mind has imagined what God has prepared for those who love him.

—1 Corinthians 2:9 NLT

When you were a child and you were handed a bowl of ice cream, you probably didn't want to stop at just one scoop. Perhaps you even handed it back and said, "I want more." How often do we still do that as adults—and with more things than just ice cream? To us, *more* is so often equated with *better*.

What do you want more of today? Money, clothes, or grownup toys, like boats, bikes, or golf clubs? Maybe it's more vacation time, more power, or more prestige. *More* is enticing, and it promises fulfillment—for a moment.

The next time you begin thinking, *I want more*, rephrase and think instead, *I have more than enough*. You have a God who loves you and a Savior who gave His life for you. You have life and breath and grace. Rest in your God who always gives you more than enough.

Father, I often deceive myself into thinking I need more, but You are more than enough.

Love to Be Loved

One thing I ask from the LORD, this only do I seek: that I may dwell in the house of the LORD all the days of my life, to gaze on the beauty of the LORD and to seek him in his temple.

—Psalm 27:4

What is it about the love and admiration of others that moves us to strive for more? Maybe it's the love of a spouse, your boss's respect, your dad's approval, or the admiration of a new friend. These aren't bad things. After all, it feels good to be admired and respected. But that feeling is addictive, and worth watching out for.

If we feel someone doesn't like or notice us, it's hard. Rejection makes us feel small and unimportant. And sometimes, we bend over backward to avoid it by making someone like us. We pick up extra work, give lots of compliments, and shine ourselves up. Simply put, we love to be loved. But we are a broken people, and sometimes love just isn't reciprocated. Instead of striving after others' love and approval, seek the Lord first. He *is* love. He sees all your flaws, all your mistakes and chooses to love you still. The Lord loves to love you—and you can rest in His approval.

Thank You, Father, for loving me, in spite of my imperfections.

The Goodness of Gratitude

I am grateful that God always makes it possible for Christ to lead us to victory.

—2 Corinthians 2:14 CEV

Thanksgiving is a day of celebration. It brings to mind turkey, mashed potatoes, stuffing, green bean casserole, the Macy's Thanksgiving Day Parade, and, of course, football. It's a day when families and friends come together to feast and to share. But above all, Thanksgiving should be a time of just that—the giving of thanks to God. And we don't have to confine our thanks to just one day, either.

Not only does thanksgiving glorify God, it also brings health to our bodies. People who practice gratitude have lower blood pressure, have stronger immune systems, and are better sleepers. They are more alert and positive and are able to be more forgiving and compassionate. Their self-worth is higher and their relationships are deeper.

Today, begin a yearlong practice of gratitude. And rest in knowing that you're not only giving your soul's praise to the Father, you're also doing good things for your body.

I praise Your name, O Lord, for You are a good God and have blessed me richly.

This Is the Day

The LORD will guide you always; he will satisfy your needs in a sun-scorched land and will strengthen your frame. You will be like a well-watered garden, like a spring whose waters never fail.

—Isaiah 58:11

In the morning, before the birds begin stirring and the stars fade into the sky, God is there. He knows the course of your day and is already providing all you'll need for it. His grace is yours before you even get out of bed. If you're feeling tired and overwhelmed, God is waiting for you to turn to Him and hand Him your burdens. If you're excited for this new day, He is rejoicing along with you. This is the day the Lord has made.

You can rest in today—whatever may come—because God is with you. He will be with you each step of the way, through the trying times, the moments filled with laughter, and all those moments in between. Today is a new day, brimming with God's promises and glimpses of His wonder. Go forth with joy and find rest in this new day.

Your presence in my life is all I truly need, Lord. Thank You for this new day.

Be On Guard

Above all else, guard your heart, for everything you do flows from it.

—Proverbs 4:23

If you've ever watched a lifeguard on patrol, you've noticed that he or she scans the water constantly. Being a lifeguard requires diligence, focus, and discipline.

Just as a lifeguard guards a pool, you need to guard your schedule diligently. Say yes intentionally and say no gently, but firmly. Refusing to let your schedule become overcrowded ensures that you have time for the people and things most important to you—and that you have time to rest.

Guarding your schedule doesn't mean excluding people from your life or never helping when asked; rather, it allows you to be more thoughtful and prayerful in what you agree to take on. It helps you avoid burnout, and it allows you to create time for rest and rejuvenation. This is actually doing a favor not only to yourself, but also to your family, friends, and community. Because the more rested you are, the more you're able to give yourself to them.

Father, I offer up my day to You. Show me what You would have me do.

Healing on the Inside

The LORD is good, a refuge in times of trouble. He cares for those who trust in him.

—Nahum 1:7

Recovering from illness or injury takes time. And though the progress may not always be readily apparent, slowly and surely, the body does heal. And, after a while, the glow of health and strength returns.

The same can be said about a person in need of physical and spiritual rest. If you have been worn down by the demands of this life, remember that recovering from deep exhaustion takes time. And though the progress may not always be readily apparent, slowly and surely, your body and your spirit will heal.

As you begin to rest and recharge, and as you lean on the Lord, you'll find your inner strength returning. Your shoulders slowly relax. Your eyes begin to shine. You laugh more easily. Don't be discouraged if the process takes more time than you'd hoped. The Lord is working in you to heal you, to give you rest, and to fill you with His peace that passes all understanding.

Father God, restore my body and my soul to a place of restful peace.

The Lord Has Been Good

The LORD is gracious and righteous; our God is full of compassion. The LORD protects the unwary; when I was brought low, he saved me.

—Psalm 116:5–6

The psalmist says, "Return to your rest . . . for the LORD has been good to you" (v. 7). Because of the Lord's goodness, we can find rest for our souls. We can set aside all worries and striving, all that is wrong in this world, and rest in the graciousness, righteousness, and compassion of our God. In Him—and in Him alone—we can find true rest.

Find comfort in these words today. The Lord is good to those whom He loves, which means He's good to you! He delights in lavishing you, His child, with love. And He desires to bring rest to your soul.

Is your soul at rest today? Do you feel uneasy about life's circumstances? Do you feel disconnected from God? Call out to Him. Run to His strong arms, for the Lord is looking on you with love and compassion. He is good, and He will give you rest.

Lord, You are so good to me, and I turn to You for rest.

Boundaries in a Busy World

The name of the LORD is a fortified tower; the righteous run to it and are safe.

—Proverbs 18:10

Imagine you're walking down a busy sidewalk. What would happen if you suddenly stopped and sat down to rest right in the middle of the sidewalk? You'd probably get bumped and knocked around. It wouldn't feel particularly restful because you'd be distracted—by the threat of imminent trampling!

That's often how it feels when we try to rest in this busy world. There's just so much going on. We sit down to pray, and the phone rings. We close the door, and someone knocks.

How can you sit still and find rest without getting trampled? First, get off the sidewalk. That means you need to set boundaries and make your times of rest clear. Tell your family. Turn off your phone. Remove distractions, and make it clear you cannot be interrupted. Then you can fully focus on being still before the Lord.

You can sit still in a busy world; it just takes some boundaries.

Help me set boundaries to that I may have time to sit still before You, Lord.

Endings and Beginnings

"Seek first his kingdom and his righteousness, and all these things will be given to you as well."

—Matthew 6:33

At the end of the month, we often wonder where the time went. Wasn't it just October? How are we already on the cusp of December? And even as we wonder, time ticks on, each second bringing us closer to a new day, a new month, and a new year.

Perhaps this year has been filled with joy. Or perhaps it has been filled with disappointments and regrets. Regardless of how the year has gone thus far, you are faced with a choice: Will you choose to let the past determine your future? Or will you choose to view this new day—each new day—as the beautiful gift of a new beginning? Because, either way, time goes on.

Why not choose the gift? Why not put the past to rest, live with joy in this moment, and look forward to the future with hopeful anticipation?

Jesus, fill me with hopeful anticipation of all the ways You'll work in my life.

DECEMBER

"I will refresh the weary and satisfy the faint."

—Jeremiah 31:25

Focus on Jesus

"Ask and it will be given to you; seek and you will find; knock and the door will be opened to you."

—Luke 11:9

It's December, and with this blessed month comes a flurry of holiday activity. Christmas parties, presents, cookies, pageants, trees, and more make their way onto our calendars and to-do lists. And in the hustle and bustle of the season, the true reason for all the celebration—the birth of Christ Jesus, our King—is often forgotten.

Christmas is full of wonderful traditions, nostalgia, and beautifully wrapped gifts, but at its heart is the story of the greatest Gift of all. This month, commit to focusing on Jesus. Remind yourself of the daily gift that He is to you. He came so that you might have life—abundant, rich, full, and everlasting. He came to conquer evil, to erase sin, and to bring redemptive grace to all who would follow Him. And He came so that one day you could go with Him to meet the Father in heaven. Rest in Jesus this Christmas—the true reason for the celebration.

This Christmas season, Jesus, keep my eyes and heart focused on the gift of You.

Worth the Wait

The LORD is a refuge for the oppressed, a stronghold in times of trouble.

—Psalm 9:9

You know that smell—warm and rich and heavy with sweetness. It's the smell of a cookie, still piping hot from the oven. When you were younger, did your mom ever tell you to wait before eating just such a piping hot cookie? Did you ever *not* listen? Perhaps when she wasn't looking, you snuck one off the cookie sheet—and you still remember how it burned your mouth! Mom told you to wait so that you wouldn't be hurt. It wasn't out of meanness; it was out of love. In the same way, when God tells us to wait, it's out of love. He knows His perfect plans for us, and He is revealing them in His own perfect time.

Now, imagine you'd waited patiently for that cookie. When the time was right, your mom handed it to you. The cookie was the perfect temperature—cool enough to enjoy, but warm enough to melt in your mouth. Moms know about cookies. And God knows about you. Rest in His plans; they're always worth the wait.

Father, remind me that even times of waiting are part of Your perfect plan for my life.

The Perfect Christmas

"Remain in me, as I also remain in you. No branch can bear fruit by itself; it must remain in the vine. Neither can you bear fruit unless you remain in me."

—John 15:4

At Christmastime, there's just so much to do: picking out the perfect tree, finding the perfect gifts, hosting the perfect party, and planning the perfect Christmas meal. These are all wonderful things, but the quest for the perfect Christmas can turn overwhelming and stressful. Lay down your need for perfection. Remember that Christ came because we aren't perfect.

Odds are, there'll be a bare patch on your tree, a misplaced gift, and at least one mishap in the kitchen—and that's okay. You can rest knowing that you, your home, your parties, and your planning don't need to be perfect. The truly perfect Christmas is one spent enjoying the blessings of friends, family, and, above all, Christ. So sing the carols, delight in the lights, eat one more cookie, and give praise to the One who gives you reason to celebrate.

May my heart be full of joy, Lord Jesus, as I seek after You instead of perfection.

A Heart of Humility

While they were there, the time came for the baby to be born, and she gave birth to her firstborn, a son. She wrapped him in cloths and placed him in a manger, because there was no guest room available for them.

—Luke 2:6–7

When Jesus came to earth, He came as a baby—a vulnerable, helpless, and oh-so-tiny baby. Jesus was born not in a palace or a mansion, but in a stable, to parents who were not rich or famous or revered. They were ordinary people, caught up in God's extraordinary plan. He didn't come as a powerful king with armor of steel and armies of men to defend Himself and defeat His enemies. Yes, the Son of God came to save the world, but He came in the humblest of ways.

What humility Christ had! He reigned in heaven, yet He came to earth not to reign, but to serve. Instead of seeking attention, He sought sinners. What a lesson to us, His people. May your heart rest in humility instead of pride; may you seek God's approval instead of man's; may you find contentment and true peace in the Lord.

Lord Jesus, You came and lived a human life to save me. Help me become humble, like You.

The Power of Rest

You will rest safe and secure, filled with hope and emptied of worry.

Job 11:18 CEV

Christmas can be busy and hectic and harried, and emotions often run high. There is certainly joy surrounding the birth of Christ, but there's also family drama, contentious relationships, and stress that can quickly turn into angry words. Dear friend, as soon as you can, arm yourself with rest.

Get a full night of sleep. Spend time alone with the Lord. Let yourself sit quietly with a book. Lose yourself in the lights of the tree. Give yourself permission to rest. Because when you are fully rested, you are able to think more clearly, love more fully, give more generously, and even hold back those angry words.

Rest is powerful and one of your greatest allies in the battle for a peaceful holiday season. It is necessary. And during this busy time, it is one of the best things you can do for yourself. Prepare yourself with rest.

Father, help me rest so that I can be loving and gracious to my friends and family.

The Light of the World

When Jesus spoke again to the people, he said, "I am the light of the world. Whoever follows me will never walk in darkness, but will have the light of life."

—John 8:12

As you travel from place to place this season, you'll see thousands—maybe millions—of sparkling Christmas lights. They're strung around trees inside homes, looped around windows and doorways, and covering lampposts and rooftops. They light up the night wherever they are.

These lights are a beautiful reflection of Jesus, the light of the world. At His birth, the angels lit up the skies with their presence and their praises. His truth chases the shadows from the darkest of places, and His promises bring light to the eyes of the hopeless.

Each time you see the glow of Christmas lights, reflect on Jesus' words: "I am the light of the world." Remember how the angels lit up the sky. Lift up your own praises to Christ, the true Light of the World. And rest in knowing that the One who made the angels sing still walks with you each day.

I rest in the light of the joy of Your presence, Lord Jesus.

The Gift of Sleep

It's useless to rise early and go to bed late, and work your worried fingers to the bone. Don't you know he enjoys giving rest to those he loves?

—Psalm 127:2 THE MESSAGE

The holidays are a time of great joy, but they can also be a time of little sleep. Last-minute shopping, hurried preparations, and changed plans may drive you well into the late hours of the night, and you may be suffering from more than a little sleep deprivation. Are you tired? Do you feel the need to rest?

Dear friend, *take time to rest*. Your greatest gift to the people around you is a joyful time together. And if you're stressed and exhausted from working yourself to the bone, that's much less likely to happen. Christmas is a time of joy and thanksgiving, and it's best enjoyed—and survived—on a full night of sleep.

Refuse to succumb to holiday stress, anxieties, or pressures of perfection. Give yourself permission to rest in these next few days. That's one of the best gifts you can give yourself.

Lord, it's easy to put off resting during the holidays. Give me the self-discipline to rest.

Good News and Great Joy

He tends his flock like a shepherd: He gathers the lambs in his arms and carries them close to his heart; he gently leads those that have young.

—Isaiah 40:11

Imagine yourself as a young shepherd out tending your sheep. Suddenly, in the dead of night, an angel appears and tells you that something that has been prophesied about for hundreds of years has finally happened: "Do not be afraid. I bring you good news that will cause great joy for all the people. Today in the town of David a Savior has been born to you; he is the Messiah, the Lord" (Luke 2:10–11).

The glory of God surrounds you, and you have been given unspeakably great news: the Messiah has come. Your Savior—your Shepherd—has been born! There will be no rest tonight as you run to find this child, the Son of God, lying in a manger.

This December, pause to gaze up at the stars. Remember those long-ago shepherds and their flocks, the heavenly host and their great news. And rest in knowing that your Shepherd has come to lead you home.

Thank You, Lord, for being my Shepherd. Help me follow You home.

Rest Now

*You'll take afternoon naps without a worry, you'll enjoy a good
night's sleep. . . . Because GOD will be right there with you; he'll
keep you safe and sound.*

—Proverbs 3:24–26 THE MESSAGE

I can do it later. *I'll do it after the holidays. I'll do it when life slows down.*
How often do we say things like this as we think about taking time to rest during the Christmas season? After all, there's just so much to do. December is one of the busiest months, and it doesn't make sense to take time out to rest. Or does it?

Dear friend, it may not look sensible, but resting is actually the most sensible thing you can do. Take time to rest today. Don't push it off until tomorrow. Don't try to wait until after the new year begins. Let your body and mind take a break—even if it's only for a few minutes—each and every day.

Drive around to look at Christmas lights, drink hot cocoa by the fire, spend time reading through the Christmas story, and take a break from shopping to enjoy a cup of coffee with a friend. Rest now, not later.

*It's easy for me to put off resting, Lord. Show me pockets of time
that I can use for rest.*

His Word Speaks

All Scripture is God-breathed and is useful for teaching, rebuking, correcting and training in righteousness, so that the servant of God may be thoroughly equipped for every good work.

—2 Timothy 3:16–17

Read that scripture again—the Bible isn't simply just another book. Yes, it was written thousands of years ago, but it's not irrelevant. Its truths are just as applicable to our lives today as they were when God's divinely inspired servants first penned them. The Bible is unlike any other book because it is "God-breathed." That means that just as the Lord breathed life into Adam, He breathed His words, His truth, and His living and active Spirit into its pages.

If you feel far away from God, or you're uncertain about where to turn or what to do, seek Him in His Word. Its words are His gift to you. And it will speak to you if you open your heart and your mind to hear. Whenever you feel lost, whenever you need an answer, turn to the Lord's Word. Find answers for your questions, strength for your journey, and rest for your soul.

Lord, when I open Your Word, please use it to speak truth and wisdom into my life.

Let God

The LORD is my shepherd; I have all that I need.

—Psalm 23:1 NLT

We all like to be in control, but in reality there is so little that we can truly control. We certainly can't control others, and we can't always control our circumstances. And, often, that's a difficult truth to swallow.

When faced with a situation we don't like—your mom isn't a believer, your dad is making poor health choices, your child is hanging out with the wrong crowd, your friend is making harmful decisions—we want to fix it. This broken world impacts those we love, but we can only do so much. We can speak with love and truth, and we can live godly lives, but then we must trust God to take care of those we love.

The Lord loves your mom, dad, child, and friend even more than you do. God takes care of even the sparrows and the flowers of the field. Rest in believing that He will take care of those you love.

Lord, I trust You with my loved ones; I know You love them even more than I do.

Call to Him

This is the confidence we have in approaching God: that if we ask anything according to his will, he hears us.

—1 John 5:14

Did you ever play the game "telephone"? You whisper a phrase in a friend's ear, they whisper it in their neighbor's, and it goes around the circle until it comes back to you—and, by then, it's usually totally unrecognizable.

Sometimes our messages get misinterpreted just as in the game of telephone. We try to send a harmless e-mail, but it comes across as terse. A simple misunderstanding escalates into an argument. It's easy to mix up messages.

But when you talk to God, there are no misunderstandings. He knows your heart and every thought that goes through your mind. He hears every word, and He understands exactly what you are trying to tell Him—even if your prayer is more tears than words. That's why you can approach God confidently. He knows what you're trying to say, and He understands what you mean when all you can do is utter His name. Rest in knowing that God *is* listening.

You are a great God who listens to Your people. Thank You for understanding me.

Stepping Away from Comparison

Whatever happens, keep thanking God because of Jesus Christ.
This is what God wants you to do.

—1 Thessalonians 5:18 CEV

The days before Christmas are dwindling, and it will be here before you know it. You're trying to experience Christ in this Christmas season, but you can't help feeling just a little discontented too. Instead of basking in the joy and fulfillment of Jesus, you find yourself comparing your Christmas to that of others.

You weren't invited to that exclusive party; your colleague received a bigger bonus; your home's lights are dim in comparison to the neighbor's; your Christmas budget is smaller than last year—the list goes on. There are so many ways to compare yourself to others and to decide that you're lacking. Don't do it, friend.

Step away from comparison this month. Maybe you need to fast from social media or make a gratitude list. Ask a close friend for prayer and accountability. Comparison is a real and pressing temptation, and Christ came to free you from it. Step away from comparison, and rest in the perfection of Christ.

Comparison comes so easily, Lord. Forgive me, and help me find satisfaction in You.

The Money Tree

"For where your treasure is, there your heart will be also."
—Matthew 6:21

Wouldn't it be great if money really did grow on trees? Then every time you needed—or simply wanted—something, you could walk outside, grab some money, and head for the store. It would certainly make that Christmas shopping list easier to handle. Life, however, doesn't work that way, and that's probably a good thing. If we had all the money we ever wanted, we wouldn't know how to rely on the Lord.

So often, it's the poorest who have the deepest trust in God. Why? Because they've seen Him provide for them over and over again. When we feel as if we're providing for ourselves, we risk beginning to trust in ourselves and in our own abilities instead of trusting in God, the ultimate Provider.

Instead of a money tree, the Lord has given you something far greater: through Christ, You've been given the gift of a relationship with the One who created the trees. Rest in that truth, and trust Him to supply all your needs.

Lord, may I fully rest in Your provision instead of trusting in my own abilities.

Singing God's Praises

Let everything that has breath praise the LORD.

—Psalm 150:6

Songs ring throughout the Christmas season. From classics like "Frosty the Snowman" to "Angels We Have Heard on High," if you pause and listen, it's likely you'll hear a carol—no matter where you are. They're constantly playing in shopping malls and on radio stations, in offices and in taxis. They're probably playing in your own home. And, more than likely, you'll find yourself humming along throughout this December.

What would it be like to constantly have a song of praise on your lips? How would God be glorified if, instead of complaints and frustrations, you came to Him with thanksgiving and praise?

Make an effort to sing praises to the Lord this week. Sing a favorite hymn or worship song. Sing it to Him with all your heart. Pitch and tune don't matter—simply make a joyful noise before Him! Praise Him in song, for a heart of joy is a heart at rest in the Lord.

May the songs of my heart bring praise and glory to Your name, Father God.

Jesus, Our Friend

If anyone is in Christ, the new creation has come: The old has gone, the new is here!

—2 Corinthians 5:17

Do you have a friend who's never uttered a bad word about you? One who would do anything for you without blinking an eye? Have you ever had a friend who always speaks lovingly, patiently, and wisely, and who has never, ever sinned? Your friends may have many wonderful, positive traits, but all have sinned and fallen short of perfection. All except Jesus.

Jesus is the perfect Friend. He'll never stab you in the back. He'll never spread gossip about you or use you to get ahead. He'll never belittle you or snap at you in anger. He'll never disappoint you. But He *will* always love you.

Jesus' friendship gives rest to wandering and hungry souls. You don't need to earn His love; you can rest fully knowing that He loves you unconditionally and perfectly. What a Friend you have in Jesus!

Your love and mercy bring me to my knees, Jesus. Thank You for being my Friend.

Glory to God!

Thanks be to God! He gives us the victory through our Lord Jesus Christ.

—1 Corinthians 15:57

When the angel appeared to the shepherds to give them the good news of Jesus' birth, it was such amazing, world-changing news that "suddenly a great company of the heavenly host appeared with the angel, praising God and saying, 'Glory to God in the highest heaven, and on earth peace to those on whom his favor rests'" (Luke 2:13–14). Just imagine the majesty and glory displayed that night and the awe of the shepherds who beheld it—the angels silhouetted against the night sky, proclaiming peace to the earth and praising God with heavenly voices.

As Christmas approaches, reflect on the praise that the angels proclaimed. They were so excited, they burst through the heavens to earth, unable to hold back their praise. Today, offer up your own praises to God; sing of His glory and might. Rest in the wonder of the gift the angels proclaimed: the coming of the King.

Lord, may my praises to You never be far from my lips and heart this Christmas season.

Quiet Your Heart

Create in me a pure heart, O God, and renew a steadfast spirit within me.

—Psalm 51:10

It's just days before Christmas. Friends and family are coming into town, the Christmas tree is spreading its magical scent through the house, and the big day is just around the corner. It's an exciting time of year.

Christmas is a celebratory holiday, but it's easy to get so swept away by it all that you enter the new year a little discombobulated and quite exhausted. That's why it's so very important for you to quiet your heart before Christmas arrives.

Reflect on the meaning of Christmas. Find time in the morning to look out on the beauty of the new day and let yourself linger in your pajamas. Take a few minutes to sit with the Lord and remember His faithfulness over the past year. Find space to simply *be* in this season that's so characterized by busyness. Quiet your heart, and welcome Jesus into the season.

Renew a quiet spirit within me, Lord Jesus.

Thriving over Striving

I would have lain down and been quiet; I would have slept; then I would have been at rest.

—Job 3:13 ESV

When a plant is thriving, it grows up healthy and strong, producing flowers, fruit, or vegetables. When a baby is thriving, he or she is gaining weight, becoming aware of surroundings, and hitting milestones. But what does it look like for you to thrive?

Understand that God *wants* you to thrive and to live life abundantly. Sometimes, thriving looks like adventure and spontaneity, while at other times, thriving means quiet and stillness and rest. If you're in a particularly busy season of life, thriving may be having a clear mind and restful spirit.

Instead of *striving* this week, ask God how He wants you to *thrive*. And remember that thriving doesn't always mean producing; sometimes it means lounging in an easy chair with a book, taking a leisurely walk in the park, or simply sitting and watching the sunset with your Savior. How can you thrive today?

You know what's best for me, Lord. Here I am; please teach me to thrive.

Seeing the Good News

When the angels had left them and gone into heaven, the shepherds said to one another, "Let's go to Bethlehem and see this thing that has happened, which the Lord has told us about."

—Luke 2:15

After the angels appeared announcing the birth of Jesus, the shepherds hurried to Bethlehem to see the newborn King for themselves. Imagine the excitement and the hope they must have felt as they searched for the baby lying in a manger. But those shepherds didn't have the Bible; they didn't know the wondrous gift of the whole story.

But you do. You know the Son of God was lying in the manger, you know His message, and you know He died and rose to life again. You don't need to see that baby with your own eyes; His truth is right in front of you in the words of the Bible. What great rest this offers you!

Jesus' birth, death, and resurrection have already happened, and He is waiting for you in heaven. You don't need to wonder and wander; you can simply rest in following His amazing plan.

Lord Jesus, thank You for revealing Yourself and Your truth to me through Your Word.

Turn Your Ear

"Anyone who belongs to God listens gladly to the words of God."
—John 8:47 NLT

The dining room is buzzing with noise and activity. There is laughter, the clinking of silverware, and Christmas carols playing in the background. But suddenly a young mother stands up and rushes out. Over all that noise, she's heard her baby crying—though no one else has heard a thing.

Just as a mother is tuned in to her child's cries, you can be in tune with the Holy Spirit. God doesn't always speak with grand plans and visible signs. Rather, He often uses the still, small voice of the Holy Spirit speaking through His Word. And it is only through practice and persistence that you'll be able to recognize it. But just as a mother is always listening for her child's cries over the noise of a party or in the midst of the deepest sleep, as you spend more time with God you'll find yourself always listening for the Holy Spirit's leadings. Turn your ear to the Lord, listen to Him speak, and find rest in His leading.

Quiet my mind so I can hear Your voice, Father. May I not miss even a whisper.

The Joy of Anticipation

The angel said to them, "Do not be afraid. I bring you good news that will cause great joy for all the people. Today in the town of David a Savior has been born to you; he is the Messiah, the Lord."

—Luke 2:10–11

As a child, you probably found the anticipation in the days before Christmas to be excruciating, with all those gifts just waiting under the tree. But now, since you're older, you're able to recognize the gift of anticipation. And with it you glimpse the exact feeling the world had as it waited for its promised Savior. The shepherds knew the Messiah was coming, but they didn't know when or understand how. Imagine their joy as they heard the angel's words; the One they'd been waiting for, the Savior, had finally come!

As you anticipate the coming of Christmas, ponder the words of "O Holy Night": "A thrill of hope, the weary world rejoices, for yonder breaks a new and glorious morn." Imagine the shepherds' long-ago thrill of hope as they rejoiced in the Savior's birth—and rest in the wonderful anticipation of knowing that Jesus will one day come again.

A thrill of hope for a weary world! Lord, thank You for the gift of Jesus.

Higher Than the Heavens

Great is your love, higher than the heavens; your faithfulness reaches to the skies. Be exalted, O God, above the heavens; let your glory be over all the earth.

—Psalm 108:4–5

God's love for you is higher than the heavens. A love that big cannot even be measured—and isn't that the psalmist's point? God's love is so vast and deep and wide and big that it simply cannot be quantified. It is impossible for our finite minds to grasp.

When you are loved that much by God, you don't need to worry or fear—not even for a second! The God whose love is higher than the heavens is *for* you and *with* you. He'll never laugh at any of your worries; instead, He wants you to bring them to Him. He'll free you of your deepest worries and most pressing fears, and He'll replace them with His peace, joy, and love. This season, remember that it was not for everyone else *but* you that God sent His Son—it was out of personal, intimate, immeasurable love for you.

Rest in His love today. It's more powerful than you could ever imagine.

Your love, O Lord, is life to me. Thank You for loving me so fully and faithfully.

The Sweetest Gift

"For God so loved the world that he gave his one and only Son,
that whoever believes in him shall not perish but have eternal life."

—John 3:16

One of the most delicious parts of Christmas is all the sweet treats. Christmas cookies, rich fudge, pecan pie, coconut cake, and a host of other delicacies line the table. Children can barely make it through dinner because they're eyeing that cookie, slice of cake, or piece of pie—and adults feel exactly the same.

Desserts feel celebratory, and what better reason to celebrate than the birth of Jesus Christ? The gifts we have received through Him are beyond our greatest imaginings. His birth brought hope to the world, His death erased our sins, and His resurrection dealt the deathblow to death.

The most delicious part of Christmas isn't found on the dessert table; the sweetest, the most real and precious gift of Christmas is the Lord Jesus Christ. Because of Him, we can find sweet rest . . . for today, for tomorrow, for all eternity.

What a Savior I have in You, dear Jesus. How sweetly marvelous is Your gift!

An Extraordinary Day

The shepherds returned, glorifying and praising God for all the things they had heard and seen, which were just as they had been told.

—Luke 2:20

It probably started as just an ordinary evening, that night the shepherds were out tending their flocks. Until . . . Mary gave birth to Jesus. Until the angels appeared and lit up the sky. Until humble shepherds met the Messiah face-to-face. Until ordinary became extraordinary.

Today, in many respects, is just an ordinary day. The sky remains blue, and the sun still rises and sets. Yet Christmas Day is, in so many ways, an *extraordinary* day. It's the day we celebrate the birth of our Savior. It's the day in which we take time to remember that God's own Son—tiny and humble and vulnerable—came down to earth because He loved the world so deeply. It celebrates the day that the world and our lives changed and our souls were rescued.

Take time today to rest in praise for a moment with the One who makes each ordinary day wonderfully extraordinary.

Thank You, Jesus, for filling each of my days with the extraordinary gift of You.

Prince of Peace

For to us a child is born, to us a son is given, and the government will be on his shoulders. And he will be called Wonderful Counselor, Mighty God, Everlasting Father, Prince of Peace.

—Isaiah 9:6

When Jesus was born, He looked like every other baby—small and helpless. He wasn't born with a crown on His head or riches in His hands or special features to mark Him as King; He was simply a baby. Yet that tiny baby was an essential part of God's plan to save the world. Born to die, He would one day triumph over death by rising from the tomb. With His life, He would defeat evil with good. But on the day He was born, Jesus was simply a baby.

And at the time, Mary and Joseph were probably reeling from His birth, the visits from the shepherds, and those first few hours of life as new parents. But imagine the peace that must have filled that stable as the Prince of Peace came to dwell on earth.

Jesus is your Prince of Peace. He is also your Wonderful Counselor, Mighty God, and Everlasting Father. And He can give you rest.

Jesus, Prince of Peace, You give peace to my soul and hope to my heart.

There Is Always Hope

Christ is faithful as the Son over God's house. And we are his house, if indeed we hold firmly to our confidence and the hope in which we glory.

—Hebrews 3:6

As you look toward the beginning of another year, do you feel excitement or trepidation? Do you wonder what the new year will bring? Will it bring heartache or joy? Will dreams come true or be dashed? There is no knowing the future, but there *is* trusting that the One who does know the future wants only the very best for you.

Dear friend, God is in control. And because He is in control, there is always hope. Even if your path doesn't seem clear now, He knows the way. He's writing your story—and it's a story full of grace and mercy and redemption, a story for your good and for His glory.

Lean on God; let Him fill you with His promises. He loves you and cares for you. He is trustworthy. He is good. Rest in knowing that with God, there is always hope.

Lord, as I face the future, may my hope be fully fixed in Your promises to me.

He Is with You

This is what the LORD says—he who created you, Jacob, he who formed you, Israel: "Do not fear, for I have redeemed you; I have summoned you by name; you are mine."

—Isaiah 43:1

When God tells you not to fear, He also tells you why you need not fear: He is with you; He is your God; He will come to rescue you; He will take hold of your right hand; He has redeemed you.

And one thing we know to be true is this: when God makes a promise, He keeps it. Always. Every time. Let that be of great comfort to you. God doesn't just offer empty words; He means every word He says. He gives you His presence. He is your salvation and your redemption. God gives big promises, and He keeps them in big ways.

With God on our side, we are strong. We can stand boldly, with complete confidence before any adversary. Find great hope in that today, dear friend. Find rest. For God is with you, and there's no need to be afraid.

I praise Your name, Father, for You always keep Your promises.

Give Grace

*He is the Rock, his works are perfect, and all his ways are just. A
faithful God who does no wrong, upright and just is he.*

—Deuteronomy 32:4

As you reflect on this past year, you may see things in your
life that you'd like to do differently in the coming year.
Perhaps, like so many, you make resolutions: *I will do this. I
won't do that.*

Reflecting and resolving are good, but as you do, be
sure to give yourself some grace. Don't just beat yourself
up over past mistakes, *what-ifs, I-should-haves,* or *could-have-
beens.* Instead, remember all that you did achieve this year.
Rejoice in relationships restored, friendships made, bad
habits broken, and good habits nourished.

Today, think through the many blessings of this past
year, and focus on all that was good. Rest as you give yourself grace. After all, God does.

*Remind me of the good moments of this year, Lord, and of the
greatness of Your grace.*

He Holds the Future

We live by faith, not by sight.

—2 Corinthians 5:7

The Maker of the stars and the heavens, the One who formed the trees and the mountains, the God who breathed life into man—He is the One who holds your future. He is creative. He is strong. He is almighty and all-powerful. And He loves and cares for you.

His plans may not always make sense to you, and the path you're on may feel foreign. Perhaps life has surprised you with all its joys and sorrows. But the Lord knows your every moment, every thought and desire; He rejoices in your joys and counts your every tear. And His faithfulness shines each evening in the majesty of the setting sun.

Child of God, rest assured: your future is in good hands—the Lord's hands. Only He is able to turn night into morning, sorrow into dancing. Find rest in getting to know the God who holds your future. He is trustworthy. He is good. And He is able.

I trust You, Lord my God, to lead me and guide me on this path home to You.

An Offering

*So here's what I want you to do, God helping you: Take your
everyday, ordinary life—your sleeping, eating, going-to-work, and
walking-around life—and place it before God as an offering.*
—Romans 12:1 THE MESSAGE

Do you want to know what the very best New Year's resolution is? It's life changing, but it's also a source of rest.
You don't have to do it all on your own, and it will transform you more than any diet or exercise ever could. What
is this resolution?

Put your life in God's hands.

Give Him all of it: your hopes and dreams, your fears
and struggles, your plans and failures, the big things and
all the little, everyday things. Instead of resisting His
transformation in your life, welcome it. Let go of control,
and let His power work in your life.

It may feel scary, you may feel vulnerable, and at times
you'll want to take it all back. But here's the best part: God
is transforming you every day. And every day you'll become
a little more like Jesus. It's not a quick fix; it's a lifelong
commitment. Put your life in God's hands, and rest in
knowing that He's in control.

*Lord, I put my life in Your hands; make me a little more like Jesus
each day.*

Scripture Index

Scripture Index

Scripture Index

Scripture Index

Scripture Index

Scripture Index

Scripture Index

Scripture Index

Scripture Index

Scripture Index

Scripture Index

Scripture Index